Cambridge Elements

Elements in the Philosophy of Martin Heidegger
edited by
Filippo Casati
Lehigh University
Daniel O. Dahlstrom
Boston University

HEIDEGGER ON RELIGION

Benjamin D. Crowe
Boston University

Shaftesbury Road, Cambridge CB2 8EA, United Kingdom

One Liberty Plaza, 20th Floor, New York, NY 10006, USA

477 Williamstown Road, Port Melbourne, VIC 3207, Australia

314–321, 3rd Floor, Plot 3, Splendor Forum, Jasola District Centre, New Delhi – 110025, India

103 Penang Road, #05–06/07, Visioncrest Commercial, Singapore 238467

Cambridge University Press is part of Cambridge University Press & Assessment, a department of the University of Cambridge.

We share the University's mission to contribute to society through the pursuit of education, learning and research at the highest international levels of excellence.

www.cambridge.org
Information on this title: www.cambridge.org/9781009459785
DOI: 10.1017/9781009459761

© Benjamin D. Crowe 2024

This publication is in copyright. Subject to statutory exception and to the provisions of relevant collective licensing agreements,no reproduction of any part may take place without the written permission of Cambridge University Press & Assessment.

When citing this work, please include a reference to the DOI 10.1017/9781009459761

First published 2024

A catalogue record for this publication is available from the British Library

ISBN 978-1-009-45978-5 Hardback
ISBN 978-1-009-45981-5 Paperback
ISSN 2976-5668 (online)
ISSN 2976-565X (print)

Cambridge University Press & Assessment has no responsibility for the persistence or accuracy of URLs for external or third-party internet websites referred to in this publication and does not guarantee that any content on such websites is, or will remain, accurate or appropriate.

Heidegger on Religion

Elements in the Philosophy of Martin Heidegger

DOI: 10.1017/9781009459761
First published online: December 2024

Benjamin D. Crowe
Boston University

Author for correspondence: Benjamin D. Crowe, bcrowe@bu.edu

Abstract: Throughout his career, Heidegger explored the religious sides of life in ways that had far-reaching impacts on the thought of his contemporaries and successors. This Element examines three important stops along Heidegger's ways of thinking about religion as the risky performance of life in new spaces of possibility. Section 1 examines Heidegger's 1920–1921 lectures on Paul, while Section 2 turns to the darker period of the late 1930s, exploring how Heidegger reconfigures religion in the context of his "new inception" of thought beyond metaphysics. Finally, Section 3 takes up Heidegger's challenging discussions of the divine in several postwar addresses and essays. In each case, Heidegger argues that we must suspend, bracket, or rescind from our tendencies to order, classify, define, and explain things in order to carry out a venture into a situation of indeterminacy and thereby recast religion in a new light.

Keywords: Heidegger, Martin, religion, metaphysics, phenomenology, theology

© Benjamin D. Crowe 2024

ISBNs: 9781009459785 (HB), 9781009459815 (PB), 9781009459761 (OC)
ISSNs: 2976-5668 (online), 2976-565X (print)

Contents

Method of Citation	1
Introduction	1
1 Phenomenology of the Apocalyptic Situation	8
2 God Beyond Metaphysics	22
3 Divinity in the World	44
Concluding Thoughts	61
Works by Heidegger	64
References	66

Method of Citation

Heidegger's writings are cited parenthetically using the abbreviations listed separately after the concluding section. English translations that have been consulted are also listed in that place. In cases in which the German original and the English translation are cited in the body of the text, the citations are divided by a /. Otherwise, English translations are the author's own.

Introduction

The ancient image of philosophy as a journey, what Bonaventure calls an *itinerarium*, is quite fitting for Heidegger's life-long engagement with religion. Along his way, Heidegger initiates radical lines of questioning about the history of religious thought, while maintaining the "atheism" of philosophy.[1] The impact of Heidegger's investigations of religion has been considerable.[2] A scholarly conversation about what Gadamer calls the "religious dimension" of Heidegger's work has likewise been underway for decades.[3] Instead of providing an overview of "Heidegger on religion," here I take up just three parts of Heidegger's massive output: (1) the 1920–1921 lectures on Paul given in Freiburg (GA 60); (2) the unpublished treatises on *Ereignis* from the 1930s and 1940s; and (3) postwar essays and addresses from the late 1940s and 1950s. While these parts of his corpus are crisscrossed by commonalities and resonances, I am not claiming that they evince any sort of systematic unity. Heidegger's exploratory, experimental, and self-revising approach to philosophy defies any conventional understanding of what a philosophical system looks like. But one thing that is shared by these three moments in Heidegger's philosophical *itinerarium* is a call to suspend received conceptual frameworks and to venture a new engagement with religious life in manifold forms. Heidegger argues in his 1920 lectures on the New Testament that we must give up on a certain scientific "attitude" [*Einstellung*] and its assumptions about objectivity to understand the "sense of the performance" [*Vollzugssinn*] of early Christianity. In manuscripts and notes centering on

---

[1] For two accounts of what could perhaps best be termed Heidegger's "a-theism," or bracketing of any consideration of God within phenomenology, see Hemming 2002 and Wolfe 2014, especially chapters 3 and 4.
[2] Some of the earliest to respond to the publication of *Being and Time* (1927) were theologians, both Protestant and Catholic. See Wolfe 2014 for details.
[3] Select contributions in the development of this conversation include Macquarrie 1965, Van Buren 1994, Kisiel 1994, Coriando 1998, Crowe 2006 and 2007, McGrath 2006, and McGrath and Wiercinski 2010. Besides the first of these, this list includes more strictly scholarly treatments of Heidegger and religion, rather than Heidegger-influenced works of philosophical theology or phenomenology of religion. A bibliography of all of the original work, in various fields, that references or alludes to Heidegger's ideas about religion would surely approach an overwhelming length.

the *Contributions to Philosophy* (GA 65), Heidegger looks to overcome "metaphysics," as an inflexible explanatory schema, and to perform a "leap" into a space of indeterminacy that enables a possible reconfiguration of the relationship between the divine and the human. In postwar writings, Heidegger gestures toward such a reconfiguration, "dwelling," in the midst of the reigning "positioning" [*Ge-stell*] that places everything, including God, "on order" [*bestellbar*]. These various ways of placing [*stellen*] things, producing [*her-stellen*], representing [*vorstellen*] them, restrict the range of possibility for the actual performance [*Vollzug*] of meaningful life. As ways of setting up or adjusting into place [*einstellen*], they all stand at "arm's length" from life.

Excursus: "Performance" [*Vollzug*]

An aspect of Heidegger's thought that I want to emphasize, especially because of its relevance to his investigations of religion, is that it is, itself, performative, and that performance is the subject matter of Heidegger's explorations. The language of "performance" derives from Heidegger's usage in early lectures from 1919 to 1921, as well as in later texts from the 1930s and 1940s (see Section 2). The thematic of "performance" [*Vollzug*], which can also be translated into English as "enactment," "implementation," and "actualization" appears first in the context of Heidegger's early reorientation of phenomenology away from the model of theoretical science. What Heidegger has in mind when he discusses "performance" in a phenomenological sense has an (unacknowledged) Husserlian pedigree in the notion of intentional "fulfillment" [*Erfüllung*] in intuition. In both cases the intuition (Husserl) and the performance (Heidegger) realize or carry out (otherwise only ideal) meaning. In Husserl's case, what is intended becomes subjectively present or actual; for Heidegger, the performance [*Vollzug*] itself has a meaning [*Sinn*] or "how" that enacts a relation [*Verhältnis*] to a content [*Gehalt*]. The "how" of the performance cannot be specified or determined ahead of time (GA 60, 59–61). In the 1920–1921 lectures, Heidegger explores the "how" of early Christian life, carried out "in" the world and yet not "of" the world (GA 60, 121–122). The tendency to focus on the "what" in theorizing a domain of objects, on getting it "right," excludes this "how," and its indispensable role in the formation of a life becomes inaccessible. If we want to avoid this tendency, which Heidegger sees as built into adopting an "objective" attitude in order to secure "certainty," then, to paraphrase, we are going to have to get personal with philosophy. While Heidegger later gives up talk of "factical life," and of the threefold "senses" that collectively constitute the conditions for life's intelligibility – performance sense

[*Vollzuggsinn*], relation sense [*Verhältnissinn*], and content sense [*Gehaltsinn*] – the same cannot be said of the language of "performing" [*vollziehen*] as such. Sections 1 and 2, in particular, will bring out the importance of the performative nature of Heidegger's philosophy at different moments in his career.

Doing Philosophy *with* Heidegger

> The herdsman [*Hirt*] can ex-ist as a thinker. In that case, the herdsman is a shepherd [*Schäfer*] whose flock consists of the thoughts that are to be thought about the world. His thoughts are *sheep*, and they are as refractory as the name suggests. Sheep go astray [*irrig*]. (GA 98, 240)

> In truth, thinking is thrown into a torrent [*Strom*]; it involves a great deal of trouble and distress to remain upright in the current [*Strömung*] and not to be cast out of the stream's course [*Stromrichtung*] onto the bank. (GA 98, 241)

In these two adjacent passages in private notebooks from the late 1940s, Heidegger uses vivid images to portray what philosophy is for him. Both images suggest being forced or impelled along unpredictable courses, either by one's errant charges or by a raging river. For Heidegger, philosophy is something that one is drawn into; philosophy has a compelling force despite the risks of failure and loss that come with it. For my own part, a more redolent image of philosophy is of the public space (*agora*) in which people are called upon to give an account (*logon didonai*) of things.[4] It is from this way of thinking about philosophy – call it Socratic-Platonic – that I approach thinking through what Heidegger says about religion in the texts I am considering in this Element. To be sure, Heidegger shares with the Socratic–Platonic approach the understanding of philosophy as *performative*, as a risky venture in which everything is put at stake (see above). That is precisely what makes what compelled him still so compelling for others. There is indeed something bracingly revolutionary about Heidegger's way of doing philosophy. Such a venture could hardly fail to turn up something important. Heidegger's philosophical work in this respect could be likened to a mining drill that casts off chunks of material as it bores into a subterranean rock face, among which we can find much that is precious and valuable in surprising ways, whether or not we join in the excavation. Or, to stick with Heidegger's own metaphor, as he patiently shepherds his thoughts along the way, he leaves no lack of stray "sheep" behind that are worth being gathered in. Rather than taking on Heidegger's own project, and being swept

---

[4] Heidegger's great predecessor Husserl articulates a similar starting point for thinking about philosophy in 1923–1924 lectures on "First Philosophy." See Husserl 2019.

along in its unpredictable current, I think it worthwhile to linger over some of what this project uncovers, and to sort out what is worthwhile from what is not.

There is a general reason for why I am not aiming at faithful reconstruction of the ins and outs of Heidegger's lifelong philosophical peregrination, but at a more selective consideration of a few segments of his work. As already indicated, what Heidegger does is to inaugurate a distinctively performative approach to philosophy which he, at certain times, compares to a "leap." It is reasonable to expect to find something that *motivates* the "leap," which makes the performance perhaps mandatory or commendable. To summarize in advance some ideas that will be examined in more detail in the following sections, Heidegger's principal reason for the "leap" is that, if we fail to undertake the performance that is being called for, we are destined to inhabit a world empty of significance, simply marking time until humanity annihilates itself and its planet. This, Heidegger says, is the "emergency," "plight," or "need" [*Not*] that lends the leap its necessity [*Notwendigkeit*].[5] This is all the final legacy of the history of "metaphysics," a way of thinking that we must learn to see our way past, or beyond, or beneath. This is where a difficulty arises. One might accept that there is indeed a planetary "emergency" or "plight." Yet accepting Heidegger's account of it requires accepting his conception of metaphysics and what it entails about the history of philosophy. In various ways in the following sections, I point out that it is not unreasonable to find something dogmatic and reductive about Heidegger's schema of the history of philosophy that eventuates in the "emergency" of the present. To summarize what receives further discussion below, Heidegger largely abandons *any* conventional projects of justification, stipulating that his goal is neither explanatory nor does it aim at an improved description (see Sections 1 and 2). As a result, Heidegger does not clarify the relationship between the complex historical actuality of philosophy and the background ontological assumptions of an era in the "history of being."

Most fundamentally, I find that Heidegger's account of the history of metaphysics conflicts with the pursuit of a "destructive" retrieval or "repetition" of historical possibilities, carried out over against rigid conceptual frameworks and distorting assumptions built into prevailing intellectual attitudes [*Einstellungen*], which Heidegger at times called for (Section 1). Heidegger assumes that what a given thinker has to say about *being* is what is most significant and most worth thinking about [*denkwürdig*]. He strenuously avoids all contextualization, all

---

[5] The connection between "emergency" [*Not*] and "necessity" [*Notwendigkeit*] in Heidegger's thought, particularly from the 1930s, has been convincingly examined by Richard Polt. See Polt 2006 and 2019. I am indebted to Polt's work for gaining an understanding of this important aspect of how Heidegger does philosophy.

examination of what he sometimes called the "hermeneutical situation" of both the philosopher being investigated and the one doing the investigating (Heidegger himself). Heidegger often proceeds as though what he says in 1923, that "[p]hilosophy is what it can be only as a philosophy of 'its time,'" were not true (GA 63, 18). History, Heidegger had maintained, is not a research program, but a matter of direct personal and shared urgency.[6] But, it would seem that Heidegger's schema of "metaphysics" and its history gets in the way of actually uncovering what is valuable in the philosophical tradition. Of course, none of this amounts to a refutation in detail of what Heidegger says about the history of philosophy. There is certainly much that is worthwhile in his readings of the likes of Aristotle, Leibniz, Kant, and other key figures in the history of Western thought. My point is only that Heidegger motivates his "leap" with an approach to understanding the history of philosophy that is questionable.

What I am going to present here is at once less than Heidegger and more than Heidegger. It is *less* than Heidegger in that important commitments that motivated him are not shared. Practically speaking, this means that what follows is meant neither as an exegetical commentary on nor even a general overview of what Heidegger says about religion. I am investigating not the "whole" Heidegger, but rather three possibility-laden stops along his lengthy *itinerarium*. While what I am presenting is in this way *less* than Heidegger, it is also meant to be *more* than Heidegger. Heidegger himself often describes his own thought as a series of "pointers," "indications," "hints," and "gestures" meant to draw attention to an experiment of thinking that must be performed. In the spirit of these insistent suggestions, I pursue lines of thought that Heidegger himself does not explore, but which he, at times, seems to point out. The chief example of following up such hints in what follows starts from the recognition that the three bodies of work on which I draw for my investigation differ in an important respect. As will be explored in Section 1, in his 1920 lectures on Paul, Heidegger undertakes to suspend objectifying and classificatory "attitudes" [*Einstellungen*], and in this way to indicate the shape of the performance of a unique religious life. The acknowledged difficulty of carrying out this intellectual task is at least somewhat eased by the presence of an exemplar, a *text*, that would constrain the interpretation, namely, some of Paul's letters in the New Testament.

By contrast, as Sections 2 and 3 make plain there is no such exemplar for Heidegger's equally radical philosophical experiments from the 1930s into the 1950s. Heidegger is trying to indicate something that escapes the grasp of metaphysics and of technological "positioning [*Ge-stell*]." But there is no text there guiding his reflections, no example of the sort of thing he is trying to

---

[6] I examine Heidegger's earlier approach to the history of philosophy in Crowe 2006 and 2019.

indicate, which is, after all, the outcome of a creative "leap [*Sprung*]." Fortunately, Heidegger does turn out to give at least *some* indication of what he is talking about in materials added to the published version of his important postwar address, "The Thing." There, in response to an inquiry, Heidegger says that "divinity" [*die Göttliche*] is exemplified by its presence "in Greek culture [*Griechentum*], in prophetic Judaism [*Prophetisch-Jüdischen*], in the preaching of Jesus" (GA 7, 185). In Sections 2 and 3, I follow up the second and third of these suggestions in order to articulate a richer understanding of the possibilities opened up by Heidegger's thought, in both cases drawing on biblical texts, in something like the way Heidegger had done in 1920.

Excursus on Nazism

> Today there are plenty of people who think that, because Hitler and his henchmen were crushed by the International, the eternal truth of Christianity has been confirmed. One takes the international to be the incarnation of morality; one thinks it is evidence for faith if an ecclesiastical regime and its faith are thrust into power. (GA 98, 21)

Read in isolation, for the first time, by a person with a basic understanding of the major events of the twentieth century, these lines could be read as a warning against moral complacency on the part of the victors in the Second World War. If it were recalled that this was written in a world on the brink of radical upheavals like globalization and decolonization, unfolding beneath the shadow of nuclear annihilation, then the warning being issued by the writer might even be taken to be salutary. In point of fact, however, the author of these lines was a noted supporter of "Hitler and his henchmen," who, beyond scattered, obscure remarks, never had much to say after the fact about what he had participated in. Looked at again in light of this news, these lines give off the whiff of evasion and misdirection, of an attempt to dodge responsibility by casting aspersions elsewhere. In this manner, these lines from the notorious *Black Notebooks* epitomize the problem of Heidegger. On the one hand, his criticisms of modern culture and his calls for authenticity, alongside the depth and rigor of his philosophical inquiries, mean that Heidegger demands our attention. On the other hand, the indisputable fact that he put his intellectual gifts in the service of a hideous regime rightly repels many people from examining his thought carefully or even at all. To be sure, much has been written, and needs to be written still, about the problem of Heidegger.[7] The

---

[7] Some of the seminal examinations of Heidegger's Nazism, while they succeeded in prompting much needed reflection and some important work, unfortunately have a tendency toward the sensational or tabloid-esque. These include Farias 1991, Faye 2005, and Trawny 2015. For a contrastingly sober and exhaustive examination of Heidegger and the Nazis, see Zaborowski 2010.

conversation on Heidegger and Nazism is far from over, and a great deal remains to be thought through and articulated. I am going to argue in this Element that Heidegger provides resources that help us read an indelibly Jewish book (i.e., the Bible). The fraught nature of this undertaking is apparent given Heidegger's serious involvement in the cultural politics of the Third Reich. What I am going to say in this study requires that the darker side of Heidegger be discussed, but I will limit myself here to explaining why I think that the problem of Heidegger, which is very pressing indeed, does not require ignoring what he says or foreswearing the effort to think it through.

Martin Heidegger was a convinced Nazi who failed to take any real public responsibility for that fact after the cataclysm that ended the regime. Does that mean no one should bother to read, ponder, criticize, reconstruct, or teach his work? It is difficult to see how this could be so. To demand that Heidegger be laid aside because of his politics alone seems to assume something like an "intellectual contagion" theory of the transmission of philosophical thinking. It is as if the "Nazi" or "fascist" tendencies in Heidegger's work could "infect" another person who simply thought some about what he says. It is for social scientists to investigate whether something like this actually happens or not. I will only point out that such a view of how ideas travel is part of the case that fascists of all stripes make to undermine free inquiry (remember "Jewish science" or "bourgeois historiography"?). Demanding the excision of Heidegger from the canon of European philosophy is questionable for other reasons as well. It looks to be the sort of move that is meant to establish maximum moral credentials at minimum personal cost, which in turn sounds self-exculpatory in the manner of some of Heidegger's own postwar comments. Denouncing Heidegger for his Hitlerism, in fact, buys two things in one go: a public exhibition of one's own virtue, and an excuse not to read thousands of pages of tortured German.

Is Heidegger's philosophy in and of itself "Nazi" or "fascist"? The problem with the question, thus formulated, is that "Nazi" and "fascist" are not especially precise terms. Part of what characterizes these political ideologies is that they are vague, contradictory, and equivocal. The name "National Socialism" itself is best understood not as an indicator of the party's convictions, but as a marketing strategy designed to evoke politically significant terms current at the time, and to suggest an illusory all-embracing solution to the current problems. The very fact that Heidegger could think of his own call for a "new inception" as consistent with the "inner truth and greatness" of Nazism proves the point. A workable conception of what Nazism entails is something that requires historical research, which so far has yielded an ideology held together by very little. This means that it is pointless to ask whether or not Heidegger's philosophy is "Nazi" or "fascist" in any nontrivial sense, since we have little sense for what an answer to the question would be like. It is, of course, true that Heidegger being a member of the Nazi Party means that his philosophy was authored by a Nazi, but this truth sheds little light on the respect in which the philosophy is "Nazi." Heidegger's Nazism does, however, tell us something very important about how he carries out philosophy. On the one hand, the relentless, lifelong pursuit of a fundamental inquiry to its uttermost limits is compelling on its own to many. It is hard to imagine such a pursuit being entirely devoid of valuable results. Yet Heidegger's life also demonstrates that his very distinctive brand of intellectual monomania leads to isolation, inaccessibility, excesses of abstraction, and ultimately to a simple lack of humanity.[8] What this means is that being swept away in the current with Heidegger is ill-advised, and that Heidegger's thought can most helpfully be engaged from an independent and critical position, not that Heidegger should be erased.

1 Phenomenology of the Apocalyptic Situation

> All "recourse" [*Rückgriffe*] to the past remains uncreative if it does not arise from the most extreme decisions, but only serves instead to avoid them by mixing in as much as possible. (GA 65, 52)

In his lectures on Paul (Freiburg winter semester, 1920–1921), Heidegger adopts a radical new approach to philosophy under the banner of "phenomenology" while simultaneously rejecting the basic methodological foundations of classical phenomenology. For Heidegger, philosophy investigates a performance [*Vollzug*], rather than being a description of a preexisting domain that employs the categorical framework implied by a particular "attitude" [*Einstellung*]. Heidegger holds that the actual performance of life in its concrete specificity evinces its own shape or structure, while an "attitude" cancels or annuls the performance. That the sense of life depends upon the "how" of its performance means, for Heidegger, that the phenomenology of "factical life" must itself re-perform the "how" of a kind of life. In keeping with the phenomenological motto, "to the things themselves!", the "scientific" attitude is to be suspended to recapture this "how." This way of describing what Heidegger undertakes in the 1920–1921 lectures might remind some of what he says much later, in the 1930s, as he once more attempts a "leap" [*Sprung*] (see Section 2). In his lectures on Paul, Heidegger could be thought of as deepening or broadening Husserl's phenomenological reduction by

---

[8] It can sometimes be illuminating to consider the lives of philosophers as (at least parts of) arguments for or against a certain way of approaching philosophy. For a recent example, see Millgram 2019.

rescinding from or suspending certain very basic commitments about what it means to approach philosophy "scientifically."

What Heidegger's maneuver aims to accomplish is "recalling" or re-performing a possibility of being human rather than describing it as a preexisting topical domain or object. Heidegger specifically undertakes to perform a "leap" into the *apocalyptic Situation*, the sense of which he conveys with remarkable depth and fidelity by setting aside the domain of pure consciousness that is otherwise posited by the phenomenological attitude. While this allows Heidegger to illuminate the "performance sense" [*Vollzugsinn*] of ancient Christianity, his own phenomenological re-performance is worth querying. By bracketing categorical and evaluative frameworks, Heidegger can say nothing about *why* it is imperative to grasp ancient Christianity in its performance [*Vollzug*]. Furthermore, as Heidegger powerfully shows, it belongs to the performance of living within the "apocalyptic Situation" that the performance is a *response* "in fear and trembling" to something overwhelmingly *insistent*. But any such response is curiously suspended, if not cancelled, in Heidegger's phenomenological re-performance.

1.1 Husserl's Phenomenology

There are numerous places in his writings in which Heidegger directly indicates the significance of Husserl's phenomenology for his own philosophical project, and Husserl's legacy can be discerned behind many crucially Heideggerian contributions. Different scholars emphasize different facets of this legacy in Heidegger's works, and I will not enter very far into that important discussion here. Instead, I want to stick to what Heidegger says at times about the *general* importance of Husserl's phenomenology. A recently published volume of the *Collected Edition* (volume 82) is a convenient place to find helpful remarks on this score. This fascinating volume collects Heidegger's marginalia and other commentary on his own writings, principally *Being and Time*, but also writings from the 1930s and 1940s. I single out here just one passage on the role of Husserl's phenomenology in Heidegger's philosophy, written in 1936:

> [T]he thing that is essential and can be recognized and taken on from [phenomenology] – [is] pushing forward to the "things themselves" [*Sachen selbst*]; but this must be understood in terms of its contrary – opposed to the classification of opinions, opposed to gluing together "systems" to make a worldview, opposed to "psychological" explanation. Which things are taken to be "the" things [themselves] is a secondary question – [...] this *will* is still decisive. [Phenomenology] *bears within it a driving historical impulse* [geschichtliches Stoßkraft], however

"questionable" its own historical (i.e., here [meant] historiographically) opinions must remain. (GA 82, 145)[9]

Heidegger values phenomenology because it promised something new with the phenomenological "bracketing" of objectifying frameworks. It is notable that the conceptual apparatus of phenomenological method, along with characteristically Husserlian doctrines, are conspicuous by their absence from Heidegger's recollections. What the religion lectures of 1920–1921 bring to light is that Heidegger had, in fact, long since set aside the very foundation of Husserlian phenomenology. All that remained to receive his later acknowledgment was the *impetus* to relentlessly bore down to the things themselves – leaving behind any and all "attitudes." It is precisely this element of Husserl's legacy that Heidegger had already taken up in the 1920–1921 lectures.

What Heidegger "brackets" is not an incidental feature of Husserl's phenomenology, but rather the very move that makes it possible, the shift from the "natural" to the "phenomenological attitude" [*Einstellung*]. "Attitude" is the standard English rendering these days for the German "*Einstellung*." But it is important to pay attention what Heidegger is trying to indicate with this vocabulary, which means considering the semantic range of the term he is using. To "*einstellen*" something is, at the most generic level of meaning, to position it, put it someplace, to adjust it into position. In the reflexive form, it means to take up a position oneself, for example, in a line. From the late nineteenth century, the dominant sense came to be that of taking a position relative to something in the sense of having a point of view on it, or an attitude about it. Both the older sense and the more modern one are in play for Heidegger in the 1920–1921 lectures. To adopt an *Einstellung* for Heidegger means to take up an attitude toward something that locates it within some conceptual or categorical framework.[10] An example of what Heidegger means could be seen in the classic procedure of botanists; there is a preexisting framework of taxa to which a specimen can be seen to belong, or else a new classification must be derived according to the established rules of biological taxonomy. Having knowledge here means locating the specimen in such a pre-delineated, logically ordered scheme. Taking up an *Einstellung*, such as the "phenomenological attitude," is the prerequisite for acquiring knowledge in this sense.

The *locus classicus* for Husserl's discussion of *Einstellungen* is the introduction to *Ideas I*. Husserl maintains here that, by adopting a particular *Einstellung*,

---

[9] Cf. inter alia GA 82, 30; 144.
[10] While it would be highly speculative to assert any direct linkage, it is hard not to hear in Heidegger's criticisms of *Einstellungen* his later discussions of *Ge-stell* ("positioning") and *Bestellung* ("ordering up"), as well as other terms sharing the verbal root "*stellen*." I will turn to a direct consideration of these later usages in Section 3.

by following a procedure or method of "parenthesizing," a hitherto unexplored region or domain of "being" is established and made accessible: pure consciousness. Heidegger explicates *"einstellen/Einstellung"* in a way that hews close to Husserl's usage. Heidegger explains that an *Einstellung* is specified by the manner of its *partitioning* [*Einteilung*] of the "content-sense [*Gehaltsinn*]" of experience. The point Heidegger is emphasizing is that adopting an *Einstellung* involves an already established distinction between different domains of objects.

1.2 Phenomenology against *Einstellung*

In Heidegger's lectures of 1920–1921, he emphasizes the contrast between a phenomenological approach to the subject matter and one that is *einstellungsmäßig*, "attitudinal." This point is made first made against the work of Ernst Troeltsch.[11] Troeltsch was at that time one of the most systematic and influential philosophical theologians in the world. His views about historiographical method, and the disciplinary boundaries between theology and other scientific inquiries, are still sometimes mentioned in contemporary Biblical scholarship. Troeltsch's project, according to Heidegger, is to reconstruct the essential, universal elements of religion by "assigning [religion] a place in various complexes of *subject matter* [*Sachzusammenhänge*]." To have "knowledge" [*Erkenntnis*] in this sense means to fit the subject into the logical structure of the domain (GA 60, 27). But for Heidegger, the whole aim of phenomenology is to dispense with this objectifying and classificatory approach. "That [is what] makes phenomenology so eminently difficult" (GA 60, 35–36). The difficulty is that neither the observational point of view nor the predefined domain is available for the purposes of phenomenological understanding.

The *einstellungsmäßig* approach illustrated by Troeltsch represents what it is to know something "scientifically." If one were not interested in *knowledge* about something, then the whole procedure is avoidable. But if not knowledge, what is it that is at stake in Heidegger's radicalized phenomenology? Is the payout supposed to be a refinement of our conceptual tools in the hopes of eventually having knowledge? Heidegger denies this possibility as well: "a theory of categories or a philosophical system is meaningless [*sinnlos*] from the point of view of phenomenology" (GA 60, 36). The question of what it is that Heidegger hopes to achieve with his phenomenological investigations of religious life turns out to be of critical significance. For it would seem that, in calling for the setting aside of scientific "attitudes," Heidegger is concerned to make space for a normative

---

[11] On Heidegger and Troeltsch, see Camilleri 2010.

dimension of significance [*Bedeutsamkeit*] in life, which gives matters urgency in the midst of a performance, and which is lost by adopting an *Einstellung* (GA 60, 13, *et passim*). Troeltsch typifies the consensus approach to science for Heidegger, in that he makes history – the overarching category for the study of ancient religion – a research topic rather than a matter of ultimate commitment. For to adopt an *Einstellung* is to relate to something in such a way that one's actual stance or comportment [*Verhalten*] "disappears" or "vanishes" into the "interconnection of the subject matter" [*Sachzusammenhang*]. This is what "objectivity" amounts to, after all. In this way, as something that is being lived through, the relationship is "concluded" or "wrapped up [*eingestellt*]." Heidegger explains what he means in this, yet further, usage of *einstellen* vocabulary: To say that factical life experience is *"eingestellt"* in this case has the same sense as in the statement, *"der Kampf wird eingestellt,"* the battle is over. The purpose of adopting an *Einstellung* is the "establishment" [*Verfestigung*] of a "foundation" [*Fundierung*] upon which a scientific grasp of a subject area can be built. It makes it possible to "straighten out" or "sort out" an entire region of objects.

Heidegger declares that such an *einstellungsmäßig* procedure "*has nothing to do with phenomenological understanding*" (GA 60, 49, italics in original). In understanding something phenomenologically, there is "no inclusion within an object domain [*Sachgebiet*], but rather the opposite of this" (GA 60, 60). For the same reason, "[o]ne steers well clear of any classification [*Einordnung*], and leaves everything undecided" (GA 60, 60).[12] Without this avoidance of objectification, the living *performance* [*Vollzug*] of the phenomenon cannot happen "freely." It is this enacted, performed, carried out characteristic of life as it is lived, which always has its own particular "how," that is completely elided by the adoption of an *Einstellung*. All meaning [*Sinn*] is inseparable from this performance. As Heidegger will later maintain with respect to Paul (and Augustine), the content [*Gehalt*], i.e., God, and the relation [*Bezug*] to it, i.e., faith, are both only fully intelligible in the actual performance of the relation. The full sense of the phenomenon is only given in the *Vollzug*. Grasping the "sense of the performance" [*Vollzugssinn*] of the phenomenon requires casting aside the concern for objectivity and neutrality that characterizes Troeltsch's (and others') conceptions of science.

A seemingly obvious or natural "region" or "domain" within which to locate religion is "consciousness." After all, in a disenchanted world laid open for

---

[12] At the outset of the SS 1921 lectures, Heidegger revisits the issue of *Einstellung* and makes similar observations. An "object [*Objekt*]" is an entity that is defined by its place within an *object-complex* [*Objektzusammenhang*] that has a "generic [*gearteter*] ordering," i.e., in a particular hierarchy of categories. This "ordering framework [*Ordnungsrahmen*]" defines what is *real* or *actual*, the bearer of "all further evaluations and positions." It is in this sense that a phenomenon is not an *Objekt* for Heidegger.

scientific investigations, there is no longer anything "out there," in the world, for religion to be about. The study of religion is, as a historical science, a science concerned with what human agents make of events. Historical sciences, in this view, presuppose psychology as a more basic one. The domain of psychology – consciousness – is itself further divisible, for on the one hand consciousness is an occurrence, and on the other hand states of consciousness instantiate non-occurrent things like truth, right, and sentence meaning. But phenomenology, given what has been said already, must dispense with consciousness altogether. Up to a point, Heidegger follows Husserl's program in *Ideas I*, insofar as Husserl is concerned to differentiate phenomenology from empirical psychology, and indeed from any empirical or historical discipline. Through the phenomenological *epoche* and a series of eidetic reductions, Husserl arrives at the domain of pure, transcendental consciousness. But this way of discarding presuppositions does not go far enough by Heidegger's lights.

Therefore, despite the fact that he calls it *experience*, Heidegger's subject matter, "factical life-experience," is not to be identified with subjectivity or consciousness. The "subject," the *I*, isn't clearly distinct from the totality of factical life experience. "I experience myself in factical life as in *that which* I accomplish, undergo, and in what encounters me, in my states of depression and elation, etc." (GA 60, 13). Or, in a comment that looks ahead to *Being and Time*: "I *never experience my I in abstraction*, but rather in doing so am always caught up in [*verhaftet*] the *environment [Umwelt]*" (GA 60, 13). Experience as such has a "worldly character" in that it lays the stress on "what is significant [*Bedeutsamkeit*]," on the actual content of what's happening at a given moment (GA 60, 13). How "I" am doing at any point is a matter of being "factically caught up in what is significant in the environment" (GA 60, 14). This actuality conflicts with the tendency of philosophy toward partitioning the totality of experience.

Heidegger reconstructs in the lectures the "partitioning" process that leads up to Husserl's concept of "pure consciousness." "To the extent that a being only *exists* [*seiend*] *for a consciousness*, the *ontological* partitioning [*Einteilung*] corresponds to a *subjective* [*bewußtseinsmäßige*] one ... in which a being *is constituted*," or "comes to consciousness" (GA 60, 56). Heidegger references Kant as the first to recognize a whole new set of questions regarding this "subjective" partition, but it was left to Husserl to discover the "original laws of constitution of consciousness," and to clearly assert that "[e]verything objective [*Gegenständliche*] is subordinate to the form of this constitution" (GA 60, 57).In Husserl's phenomenology, consciousness itself becomes a region and is regarded in a way in keeping with that; its normativity [*Gesetzlichkeit*] is not only in principle original, but also it is the most universal.

This is expressed in an original and universal manner in transcendental phenomenology (GA 60, 57)."

Yet, Heidegger rejects out of hand the idea of treating the life experience of Paul and his community as a "particularization [*Vereinzelung*] of religious consciousness" (GA 60, 129). This means that the endeavor is not to recover the "representational content" [*Vorstellungsinhalte*] of the early Christians so as to reconstruct their "picture of the world" [*Weltbild*] (GA 60, 135). The whole idea of isolating the content of people's beliefs "so that they might be preserved in an eternal, *a priori* armory [*Rüstkammer*]" is foreign to phenomenology for Heidegger (GA 60, 135). Instead of adopting an attitude, phenomenology demands the "appropriation [*Aneignung*] of one's own factical *existence!*" (GA 60, 136). It is by somehow stepping into the subject matter, not sidestepping it, not externally framing it, that its real meaning can be accessed.

1.3 The Apocalyptic Situation

The life that Heidegger undertakes to phenomenologically *perform* [*vollziehen*] is first and foremost the outcome of "an *absolute reversal*" [*Umwendung*] (GA 60, 95), a complete dissolution of previous loyalties and a profound and all-encompassing reorientation of life. Heidegger observes how this reversal is not a simple inversion of values that places what was formerly reviled in the highest position, but rather the complete eclipse of all that is now deemed "worldly."[13] When the last is first, there's no longer a way to make the distinction intelligibly. Hence, the "distress" that characterizes the reception of Paul's message of the folly of the cross, which Heidegger calls the "absolute turning [*Hinwendung*] [that happens] within the performance sense [*Vollzugsinn*] of factical life," i.e., a total reorientation of life (GA 60, 95). Crucially, none of this should be framed "objectively" [*objektiv*], but in terms of how a way of life is actually performed or enacted.[14] That is, it is not *just* that people now believe different things (though surely they do); the way they actually carry out their lives has been transformed. For this reason, says Heidegger at one point, we necessarily encounter a genuine "subjective limit to understanding" in any attempt to grasp this way of life "objectively" (GA 60, 117). Or, to turn to Paul, there is no "worldly" way to break through the world as it stands. "The performance

---

[13] Heidegger observes the same kind of absolute reversal in Augustine's account of the conversion of the soul: "Through a hidden 'movement' it all comes to nothing, *inanescit* [is vanity], and everything is radically 'invalidated' relative to the *summum bonum* (before God)" (GA 60, 240).

[14] For example, the theological way of categorizing the expectation of the *parousia* under the heading of "eschatology" is something "theoretical and related to a discipline" (GA 60, 115), and so is annulled or held in suspense by the phenomenologists' drive for the "things themselves," in this case the sense of living in this expectation.

[*Vollzug*] surpasses human power. It is inconceivable [*undenkbar*] on the basis of one's own power. On its own, factical life cannot bring forth the motivation" to completely transcend the worldly horizon (GA 60, 122).

For Heidegger, a "reversal" like this cannot be understood properly within a pre-partitioned domain (e.g., "consciousness"). Instead, we must start over, he says, with "the Situation." The Situation is a meaningful whole whose parts cannot be adequately characterized independently of one another or of the *performance* or *enactment* [*Vollzug*] of the Situation as a whole. The Situation should therefore be seen as moving in a specific way, as unfolding, rather than being simultaneously available as a whole. This moving, unfolding totality contains distinguishable "directions of sense" [*Sinnrichtungen*]. Like intentional acts in Husserlian phenomenology, these serve the constitution of the total sense [*Sinnganzheit*] of the Situation. The key point, however, is that these "directions of sense" not be assimilated to conscious acts or psychological processes. To use a rough analogy, they are more like the individual plot lines in a work of literature, which have a meaning of their own while all together comprising the meaning of the whole work. For example, in his lectures on Thessalonians, Heidegger comments on how Paul's "with-world" [*Mitwelt*] isn't his *experience* of other people, but an actual relationship with other people who belong together with him to the Situation, who are part of the Situation not in the sense of objects in it but as the ones who are there with him. But this isn't to say that how he "relates" to them, his attitude about them, *isn't also part of the Situation*. Moreover, the text of his letter also makes partially accessible to us *how the Situation with them is going for him.* All of these are different "directions of sense" in Paul's Situation, not mental activities belonging to "pure consciousness."

The Situation, then, is analogous to a significant moment in a novel in which these meaningful plot lines intersect. The specifically *apocalyptic* Situation, however, reveals something of crucial importance. Paul's specific Situation, which he shares with the communities he helped to found, while itself a "totality of meaning," is a moment in a much, much larger "totality of meaning." In something like the way "Paul" and "the Thessalonians" are *in* the Bible, in the sense of being characters who occur within a story, Paul and the Thessalonians are *in* a meaningful process that they at best comprehend "in a glass darkly," though important clues about it have been *revealed* – hence, it is "apocalyptic." The *apocalyptic Situation* is one in which every intelligible stance on the world meets with and is overtaken by something that permanently exceeds it. In the apocalyptic Situation, one has been exposed to a perspective that encompasses every human perspective and goes beyond it. Life has a new direction that it would never have discovered on its own. The entire "form" or *schema* (Paul's

Greek in Romans 13) of the world is passing away, and a new or renewed world – not a new outlook on the world, but *a world* – is taking its place.

In characterizing the Situation as "apocaplytic," I am adopting a common term (also current in Heidegger's day) to refer to a certain distinctive way of viewing life that emerged within the larger framework of ancient postexilic Judaism. It has been more or less agreed since before Heidegger's lectures on Paul were given that this approach to life was a significant part of the milieu in which Christianity came into being. The term itself comes from the only self-proclaimed "apocalyptic" text, Revelation (*Apokalypsis Ioannou*), the final book of the Biblical canon, but it is applied to both Biblical (Daniel) and non-Biblical (1 Enoch, 4 Ezra, 2 Baruch) texts. What is most important for my discussion about the apocalyptic point of view is how it operates to enable the construction of a different way of seeing things, and in particular of the ultimate decision points in life, which are schematically represented as pairs of opposites that are arrayed both spatially (heaven, earth) and temporally (injustice, future judgment). What this amounts to is stated most directly by Nikelsberg and VanderKam: "One sees the human situation both as it is and in terms of what it is not."[15] Apocalyptic writing conveys God's perspective, as it were, disclosing the hidden interrelationships between all things. John J. Collins captures this feature of apocalyptic writing in terms of the multidimensionality of the world it portrays. The meaning of events is truly seen in the intersection between the ordinary or "natural" and the cosmic and heavenly. Collins notes that, in this way of seeing things, the heavenly – which is hidden – is what is paradigmatic for the earthly (e.g., in the figure of the "Son of Man"). In this way, apocalypticism inverts what most of us would recognize the "common sense" point of view.

Apocalyptic writing opens the events of the here and now to a larger whole that is profoundly different. At the same time, the language of these texts is multivalent. The scale of things – again, both temporally (creation, the Flood, the final judgment) and spatially (the heavens, distant parts of the earth) – makes it hard to fix the sense of the text by tying it directly to a specific historical event. Rather than offering a literal description of events or of hidden aspects of the world, the narrative of an apocalyptic text is a *schema* or framework of meaning that is meant to be taken up into the life of a community.[16] The futural orientation of all apocalyptic writing – the depiction of the coming of a final judgment and

---

[15] Nikelsburg and VanderKam 2001, 41.
[16] "Apocalyptic is concerned to understand how the present relates with both the past and the future. The absence of any concern with the details of life in the future and the rather prosaic accounts of the whole of history suggest that it is not the way in which the righteous would spend their time in the kingdom but the meaning of existence in the present in the light of God's activity in the past and his hoped for acts in the future which dominated their understanding of existence" Rowland 2002, 189.

eschatological restoration – is of course one of the features that passes over into the texts of the New Testament. This is something that Heidegger perceptively accentuates in his lectures. Here too the multivalent, non-referential quality of the language is important. Apocalyptic writers reappropriate ancient mythological images and plot lines, such as divine combat with personifications of death and chaos.[17] An analogy could be drawn in this respect between apocalyptic texts and tragic dramas. By opening up a cosmic perspective on mundane history, the tensions in the latter are intensified to a point of crisis. The scene of final judgment points to a reconciliation or resolution of the crisis on an equally vast scale. What the early Christians added was a further deepening of this sense of urgency by proclaiming that the great eschatological consummation is in fact underway in the very midst of mundane history.

Long after the 1920–1921 lectures, Heidegger speaks of how notions like transcendence and being-*in*-the-world [accent on *in*] from his work in the later 1920s pointed ahead to his later conception of the "open between" in which Dasein "is arrayed" [*sich vergefügt*] or "arranged" like beams in a mortise joint [*die Fuge*], and I think this is a helpful guide for thinking about what he means by the "Situation." Heidegger's thought here isn't that subjects have a conception of the world into which things are made to "fit" – the Situation isn't an "experience." Instead, it's a place where vectors intersect. One is "joined" or "fitted" to another. Things, events, people are thus "gathered" into their places. As he puts it: "The unity and simplicity of these primordial relations is the fit that fits everything and in each respective case determines what the fitting [*Fug*] is. We call the fit [*Fuge*] historical being [*Seyn*], within which every entity unfolds" (GA 52, 100). In the apocalyptic Situation, one is *re-fitted* into the structure of God's plan of creation, which was at best only partially known previously. What Heidegger tries to accomplish in these lectures is to somehow enter into the *actual life of the Situation*, not into the belief system of some ancient people or into the historical context of the first century or the hypothetical sources of the New Testament text. The latter are, after all, not the topics of Paul's letters, they are not the "things themselves." Paul is writing about how it's actually going, in real life, in the apocalyptic Situation, for him and his community. When he speaks of "tribulation" and "expectation," he's not describing attitudes or feelings, but saying something about the way life in the world is *actually* going. It is the Situation of Paul and his community that demands that Heidegger break out of the *einstellungsmäßig* approach (Cf. GA 60, 181).

---

[17] See Ricoeur 1995, especially pp. 60–65, on how the prophetic discourse in the Bible "desacralizes" nature and social power, as supposedly "natural." Apocalypticism comes *after* this de-sacralizing, and self-consciously appropriates mythic imagery to point to further dimensions of meaning hidden in ordinary life.

Heidegger scholars are familiar with the "diagrams" of primitive Christian life that are included in volume sixty of the *Collected Edition*.[18] A passage from the lectures on Augustine has, to my knowledge, been less widely discussed, but I think it helps to make somewhat more concrete what I'm getting at. The text is a set of notes Heidegger made on one of Augustine's sermons. Heidegger comments on how Augustine invokes the cross, and its intersecting vectors, as a symbol of the life of faith. What interests him is what Augustine does to develop the notion of a life as something with dimensions *of meaning*, in addition to spatial and temporal ones. *Latitudo* – the breadth of the crossbeam, stretched open, outward facing – indicates a "richness" and "perfection in good works." *Longitudo* – the upright post stretching up from the ground – captures "patience and perseverance"; its *altitudo* or skyward directionality signifies the "expectation of what lies beyond [*über*] you (*sursum cor*)." Lastly, there is *profundum*, the depth of the upright beam in which it disappears from view beneath the earth, which supports the entirety: *quae terrae defixa est*. This, Augustine says, is the grace and mercy of God, a hidden depth that inexhaustibly grants new life from death. Heidegger's gloss on the whole passage: "All of this is not to be understood as object symbolism, but rather related back to the performance sense [*Vollzugssinn*] of life" (GA 60, 290). What Augustine is trying to indicate is the *shape of a life*, understood not as an individual's experience or worldview nor as an exemplar of a sociological category nor as a causal process. Life in its "performance sense" emerges from an inexhaustible and hidden direction, and it unfolds into a space of engagement, action, and relation characterized by breadth or openness. This space or Situation is not just *there* – it is not a state of affairs to be studied and catalogued under whatever "-studies" header might be deemed appropriate – but it is something that is demanding, insistent, *normative*. Its demandingness derives from multiple directions of relationship and is not simply a matter of personal or individual importance. For instance, in Paul, the demand can come from the side of the "world," from the values, institutions, and their supernatural sponsors ("powers and principalities"), of his time and place. Or, it can come from the shortness of the "time," or from "above," from an entirely different "kingdom" or *civitas*. The point, as Heidegger explains in the lectures on Paul, is not to get one's "hold" on life, though it is not incorrect to say that what is at stake is the meaning of one's life. Rather, the point is to be radically exposed to others and to the Wholly Other in a way that permanently de-authorizes the "world."

---

[18] This important material was first introduced in Sheehan 1979, and further explicated in Kisiel 1993.

1.4 Phenomenology *in* the Situation

So far, I've described what Heidegger found promising in Husserlian phenomenology, what he found problematic, and what it is that he apparently aimed to understand through a radically revised phenomenological approach. What, if anything, does Heidegger say by way of a positive characterization of his own approach? What he does manage to say is very suggestive, despite a certain inchoate quality, and his comments are worth exploring some more. In the 1920–1921 course, he maintains that, instead of adopting an "attitude," phenomenological understanding requires that the investigation be "subordinated to the historical Situation." For this reason, the concepts that are articulated by the investigation must possess a "labile" quality; they are *revisable*. Indeed, these "formal indications," as he famously calls them, are not properly *concepts* at all. That is because what must be "achieved" or "acquired" [*gewinnen*] is the *actualization* or *performance* [*Vollzug*] of the Situation, the actual way it unfolds as a meaningful whole when seen *from within*. The goal is not classification, not "scientific knowledge" in either Troeltsch's or Husserl's senses.

Achieving the authentic *Vollzug* of the Situation demands a repetitious specification of its facticity or givenness, as opposed to the formation of a general concept or category [*Sachbegriff*]. A constant "reversion" – or "reconversion" (?) – *Umwendung* – to the Situation is indispensible. Furthermore, it is crucial to recall that "Situation" here is not a class term, nor a category, and it therefore cannot function to organize objects in a domain. The Situation involves nothing *ordnungsmäßig*, says Heidegger. "We cannot project a Situation into a definite domain of being [*Seinsbereich*], not even 'consciousness.' We cannot talk of the 'situation of point A between points B and C'" (GA 60, 91). Later, Heidegger references the necessity for a "turning" [*Wendung*]" from what is given as an "object-historical complex [*Zusammenhang*] of events" to the originally "performative-historical" [*vollzugsgeschichtlich*] Situation. One must somehow be brought from possessing some historical information to having "transferred oneself into" [*Sich-hinein-Versetzen*] the actual living of the Situation (GA 60, 147; 95–96). "Situation" is, again, not a category or class term, but a "phenomenological *terminus*" (GA 60, 147). How, then, to achieve an understanding of the *performance* of a Situation? Heidegger says that "its own performance makes understanding difficult; this difficulty grows constantly the nearer it approaches the concrete phenomenon. It is the *difficulty of putting oneself into another's place* and it cannot be replaced by imagining oneself into it or 'vicarious understanding'; what is required is *an authentic performance*" (GA 60, 70).

It is at this point, after having at least a general picture of what Heidegger is trying to find out in his lectures on Paul and Augustine, that I want to raise a question for Heidegger about this phenomenology of performance [*Vollzug*]. Heidegger appropriates the "tendency" or "thrust" of phenomenology to capture the very *performance* of the apocalyptic Situation, and repetitively comments on the need to avoid objectification. This performance is, as Heidegger is well aware, a response to something that is in fact overwhelmingly insistent. The apocalyptic Situation demands a decision, for it lays bare questions about one's ultimate loyalties. Not deciding, or suspending decision or commitment somehow, is precisely a failure to fully live in the Situation in the way that befits it. To remain a mere observer is to completely misunderstand the nature of the apocalyptic Situation. Heidegger knows all of this; indeed, his lectures of 1920–1921 evoke the truly revolutionary nature of ancient Christianity to a remarkable degree and in a way that remains worth returning to repeatedly. The "knowledge" that Paul and his community share (about the *parousia*) is *lived* or *performed* by "serving [God]" and "enduring patiently"; it simply doesn't exist "on its own" in abstraction from this totality (GA 60, 123–124). But what should be said about Heidegger's own sojourn among the "things themselves" in these lectures?

Why are there lecture courses from Heidegger on Paul and Augustine? Heidegger's answer is problematic in light of his own philosophical revolution. There are at least two places in the text in which this question is addressed. In the first, Heidegger implicitly answers the question as to why he's giving a philosophy lecture about Paul. 1 Thessalonians, he observes, "was written in the year 53 A.D. (or some twenty years after the crucifixion); it is the earliest document of the New Testament" (GA 60, 87). This answer could be the beginning of a longer answer to a *different* question than the one I asked about Heidegger, perhaps to the question "why is a historian of early Christianity interested in 1 Thessalonians?" But, Heidegger insists, he is not pursuing the history of early Christianity, but its phenomenological reperformance. Could there be another reason why the (still widely seen as) earliest document of the New Testament is the subject of a philosophy lecture course? Heidegger eventually tries this out:

> Genuine philosophy of religion does not arise out of preconceived notions about philosophy and about religion. Rather, it is on the basis of a determinate religiosity – for us, the Christian [religiosity] – that the possibility of philosophical comprehension is made available. As to why our reflections shine a spotlight on Christian religiosity is a difficult question; it can be answered only if the problem of historical contexts [*Zusammenhänge*] is solved. The task is to achieve a genuine, original relationship to history, which must be explicated on the basis of our own historical situation and facticity. What

matters is what the meaning [*Sinn*] of history might imply for us; here the "objectivity" of the historical "in itself" disappears. There is only a history on the basis of the present. The possibility of a philosophy of religion can only be taken up in this manner. (GA 60, 125)

Why is Heidegger lecturing on Paul and Augustine? He initially seems to *defer* any answer. Instead, he suggests that there is another problem, itself only named and not explicated, that needs to be answered for there to be an answer to this question. But then he reminds us that what is at stake is not intellectual curio-collecting, but *meaning* [*Sinn*]. The meaning in question is presumably the meaning of life, understood as something that is lived in a given historical context with its own uniquely insistent demands. Here, Heidegger seems to be saying that it is not for the sake of objective historical knowledge about early Christianity that we study these texts, but instead because there may be something significant for life about what they present. Put differently, the reason to examine Paul and Augustine in this manner is that what they have to say might make a difference to your life. The Situation demands a full performance [*Vollzug*], and it is only a meaningful totality as something that is carried out. As he says by way of conclusion, philosophy too is something that has to be understood by being carried out. Heidegger makes it very clear that he is not interested in scientific knowledge about religion or its history. He also plainly rejects Husserl's quest for a science of the primordial domain of pure consciousness. The reason that these options are excluded is that, at the end of the day, they abstract from the essential performance sense of the phenomenon. The performance sense of life in the apocalyptic Situation involves life-altering commitment in response to something overwhelmingly insistent. But where is this insistence in Heidegger's account? And, more to the point, where is the commitment, one way or the other? A performance of the apocalyptic Situation as a mere historical possibility falls short of being a genuine enactment of it. Instead, it begins to seem that once again, what is at stake is something like *einstellungsmäßig* knowledge of a historical reality, albeit by way of a curious kind of *Einstellung*. Historical studies of Biblical criticism often make the observation that nineteenth-century historicism and positivism seemingly foreclosed on the possibility of there being any normative claim on the part of the Bible. This comports with an emphasis on scientific objectivity. As Walter Brueggemann, a leading exponent of "Old Testament" theology, puts it: "all of the oddness of the biblical witness has to be explained away or made to fit with the prevailing modes of what is deemed to be reasonable."[19] What is strange, however, is that Heidegger winds up suspending the normative claim

---

[19] Brueggemann 1997, 17.

2 God Beyond Metaphysics

> Metaphysics is neither a doctrine nor an opinion, nor is it the basic position of the person who is thinking; rather, [it is] the *truth of beings* (GA 67, 33).

> [A]ll Western history and modern world history as such are grounded in metaphysics. But a future humanity is entrusted to Da-sein. (GA 49, 61)

From early in his philosophical *itinerarium*, Heidegger queried the relationship between metaphysics – in the sense of the "science of being" established by Aristotle – and the Christian religion.[20] Heidegger maintains that, insofar as metaphysics came to comprise the philosophical framework within which thinking about God unfolded over the centuries in Europe, it has produced a distorting effect.[21] Already by 1920, his reading of Luther's works solidified this thought in Heidegger's mind.[22] By the middle of the next decade, Heidegger had come to see metaphysics as inextricably entangled in the spiritual history of Europe, and so in what he perceived as the "emergency" or "plight" [*Not*] of the era of technical rationality. "Metaphysics" is a label for the hidden destiny of European humanity, running like a subterranean stream beneath empirical, "surface" history. "Western humanity," he says at one point, "is in every way sustained and guided by metaphysics, in all of its comportment toward beings, and so also toward itself" (GA 6.2, 309).

The critical inflection point in this history seems to Heidegger in the 1930s to have arrived in the age of machination [*Machenschaft*]. Heidegger also learns from Hölderlin during these years to voice the thought that the "gods" have now "fled," and he likewise ponders Nietzsche's proclamation of the "death of God." Modernity had seemingly brought forth, or perhaps yielded to, a new time in which the meaning of things had been reduced to their suitability for "calculation," for technical command and control procedures. In the very teeth of this nihilistic historical moment, Heidegger in the 1930s directs his inquiries toward

---

[20] In a 1920 lecture, Heidegger refers to the "disfigurement [*Verunstaltung*]" of the original Christian message through the introduction of Greek philosophical concepts (GA 59, 91). The prior semester, Heidegger mentions merely the "constraint" imposed by Greek philosophy on Christian faith, and goes on to highlight the potential of phenomenology for undoing this (GA 58, 61). Kisiel refers to a note from as early as 1917 on this subject. See Kisiel 1993, 73–74.

[21] One perspicuous summary of this point of view can be found in 1940 lectures on Nietzsche and "European nihilism" (GA 48, 49).

[22] For the early evidence of Heidegger's study of and appreciation for Luther, see GA 58, 62, 204–205; GA 60, 97, 282, 308–310; GA 61, 7, 182.

the possibility of another "inception [*Anfang*]" of philosophical thought that could open up a new fundamental conception of humanity and of being. In order to even begin to move toward this new inception, however, what Heidegger calls the "heretofore" [*das Bisherige*] must be demolished, and the framework of "metaphysics" has to be dispensed with. This, in turn, means that philosophy must start over in thinking about God.

In his unpublished writings from the 1930s and in some of his lectures, Heidegger delineates the way in which God has been "schematized" by metaphysics as "supreme being [*das Seiendste des Seiendes*]" and "first cause." On this picture, the relationship between God and humanity is causal and unidirectional. In attempting to move beyond the framework of metaphysics, Heidegger points to a different way of thinking about the relation between God and other things (including us), a more original relation of reciprocity and shared dependence on "historical being [*Seyn*]."[23] He points to a way to recover the genuine *strangeness* of God as present yet absent, as revealed yet hidden. Heidegger maintains that, in order for these possibilities to be articulated, a radically new approach to doing philosophy is required. Philosophy in this register is not a description of any being or domain of beings, and its aim is no longer explanatory. Instead, it is a creative and highly risky "leap [*Sprung*]," and it all comes down to the *performance* [*Vollzug*]. The "leap" cannot be motivated argumentatively or dialectically, but arises only from Heidegger's all or nothing portrayal of modernity as the final working out of the train of thought initiated by the ancient Greeks. The "necessity" [*Notwendigkeit*] of the "leap" comes from the "emergency" [*Not*] we face.

As in the case of his lectures on Paul from 1920–1921, Heidegger's uncompromising approach yields genuinely valuable insights. Heidegger's thinking in the 1930s opens up possibilities of thinking of God relationally. This, in turn, points to ways of recovering the meaning of the Biblical depictions of God's strangeness that will be explored in this section. Heidegger's investigations also undercut the basis of the ideological employment of religion for the purposes of securing power by removing God from the position of ultimate cause and guarantor of certainty. Heidegger envisions a way of thinking about God and

---

[23] Historical being [*Seyn*], Heidegger makes clear, is not a metaphysical principle. There is no "danger of a pan-theism or of a uni-vocal 'explanation' of beings – being is indeed unconditioned as historical being – but never merely a highest cause or 'God'" (GA 86, 239). My choice of "historical being" as a translation for "*Seyn*" is partly drawn from Dahlstrom 2013, and also stems from a general desire on my part to avoid inventing English words. Dahlstrom has since changed his view of how best to translate the difficult term "*Seyn*" into English (see Dahlstrom 2023). In order to indicate my choice, I have included the original German ("*Seyn*") in square brackets following each reference to "historical being." There are, of course, other ways to render this critical term into English.

humanity as standing in a complicated relation of reciprocity, of mutual dependence and neediness. This way of thinking about God is suggestive of some of what has been put forth by process theology, open theism, and related attempts to reevaluate the way in which God's power is understood.

But what's the price of the ticket? It would seem that it is quite steep indeed. We are being asked to accept Heidegger's conception of the "emergency" of the modern era, and to follow him in jettisoning the tradition of "metaphysics" that, he claims, grounds the "emergency" and forecloses any attempt to move beyond it. But Heidegger's conception of the philosophical tradition is not convincing in the way it would need to be to justify such a drastic move.[24] Heidegger is certainly correct to maintain that what he starts to call *Ereignis* in these years has remained hidden or unspoken in the history of philosophy.[25] It does not follow, however, that this is the result of a rigid framework operating behind the back, as it were, of great philosophers. Adopting a view of the history of philosophy such as this – which, to revert to an earlier phase in Heidegger's thought, is suspiciously *einstellungsmäßig* – tends to get in the way of appreciating what is genuinely creative in this history. This is a result that I think should be avoided.

Heidegger's conception of the "history of being" is meant to motivate the need to undertake a philosophical performance that has no precedents, no prearranged course, no obvious criteria of either success or failure. But in that case, perhaps a more apt image for what Heidegger invites us to do is that of a "plunge" rather than a "leap." When we leap, say, across a wastewater filled gutter, we can *see* the other side already, and can say *why* it is that we're doing what we're doing ("I don't want my nice shoes to get soaked," "I don't want my feet to be cold"), and can tell whether or not we've made it. Plunging is more

---

[24] See discussion in the introduction to this Element. As an example of how Heidegger's schematization of metaphysics collapses important distinctions, see § 46 of notes for a seminar on Schelling given in 1941. Heidegger contrasts his own thinking of "historical being [*Seyn*]" with the metaphysics of the Absolute in German Idealism. Heidegger interprets the Absolute as "subjectivity" or "subject-objectivity," that is, as *a* being (GA 86, 214–215). This subjectivist interpretation, however, is worth querying. For a helpful overview of more recent revisions of the subjectivist interpretation of German Idealism, see Franks 2016. According to Heidegger, the *epistemological* subject (Descartes), the *metaphysical* subject (Leibniz), the *transcendental* subject (Kant), and *self-reverting activity* or *subject-object* (Fichte, Schelling, Hegel), all seem to be conflated or reduced to a generic notion. This move does not seem totally convincing. Fichte, to take one example, often explicitly states that "the absolute I" is *not a being*, and that the activity of self-positing is not causal.

[25] Translating the all-important term "*Ereignis*" is famously difficult, having occasioned a good deal of scholarly consideration and debate. Speaking broadly, two principal options have been taken up: "event" (and cognates) and "appropriation." Sometimes these are combined: "event of appropriation." Mark Wrathall has defended a third choice: "adaptation" (and cognates). See Wrathall 2021. While possible Darwinian resonances might by judged misleading by some, I tend to find Wrathall's careful arguments highly convincing. Still, I will rely on a range of English renderings throughout these chapters.

like falling headlong, unexpectedly perhaps, toward an unknown or not envisioned destination, and the plunge may well turn out quite badly for us. Of course, as Heidegger himself powerfully argued in the 1920s, history is something that we ultimate *are* and must *carry out*, that finitude entails radical responsibility for a life that is "in each case my own" [*je meine*]. Plunges cannot all be avoided. But Heidegger's insight into the way inherited conceptual schemata can cover up or falsify this finitude applies to his own notion of the history of metaphysics. I suggest that we can appreciate this aspect of Heidegger's thought without unreservedly joining him on his philosophical *itinerarium*, if that means adopting his historical framework. What is most important is to see Heidegger's ideas as what he often says that they are: pointers to new possibilities for thinking. Heidegger is right to insist that philosophy has to be performed, in the sense of being actively and critically examined, questioned, and finally transformed, and this applies to thinking through Heidegger's philosophy as well. Heidegger's unpublished writings and notes from the 1930s (and early 1940s) turn out, when approached this way, to offer something compelling and distinctive.

2.1 Philosophy as Performance in Heidegger's Thirties

Richard Polt has recently identified a crisis- and risk-filled era in Heidegger's intellectual life as "the thirties" (roughly, 1930–1945). Polt reminds us that "we should not wipe out this element of experiment and risk" in coming to terms with the texts from this period, and should likewise steer clear of overly systematizing Heidegger's investigations.[26] Polt is rightly drawing attention to a period of profound crisis and turmoil in Heidegger's philosophical development as well as in his personal life, and his advice about how to approach this material is well taken. Others, including Polt, have and are continuing to examine the tangled threads connecting Heidegger's philosophical work in this era with his deplorable politics.[27] My immediate interest lies elsewhere, namely, in Heidegger's resort to the language of "performance" [*Vollzug*] in unpublished writings from this time. In the previous section, I tried to demonstrate the centrality of the concept of "performance" for Heidegger's early phenomenology, particularly with respect to Paul and Augustine. In his "thirties," Heidegger once again calls for philosophy to be *performed*, rather than treated like a research topic. The performative nature of Heidegger's philosophy

---

[26] Polt 2019.
[27] Important studies of the issues involved here include Zimmerman 1990, Bambach 2003, and Thomson 2005.

during the "thirties" is an important part of what makes it so surprising and so enigmatic.

Understanding what Heidegger says in the "thirties" about God, the gods, the "last god," and the like requires recognizing that these terms do not refer to "concepts" in the usual sense; they do not add up to comprise a theoretical representation of some domain. For example, the phrase "the last god" is not descriptive of a being, different from, say, the "next to last god." These designations are rather pointers to what Heidegger called in the early 1920s the "sense of the performance" [*Vollzugssinn*] of a cluster of relations that – in the performance itself – constitute the meanings that things have for us. When Heidegger talks of the "neediness" of the god and the "guardianship" of human beings, he is not ascribing predicates to things. "Neediness" is not being added to the list of divine attributes. What Heidegger is talking about is a pattern of relationships – a multisided *encounter* [*Entgegnung*] – that as yet remains a mere possibility. In 1920–1921, Heidegger had delineated a complex of overlapping "worlds" – self-world, with world, surrounding world – a network of relations that mediate the meaning or significance of things. This meaning passes over from possibility to actuality, or is properly "constituted," through the actual performance of a life within these overlapping worlds. In the "thirties," as in the early 1920s, Heidegger once again accentuates the necessity of such performance, this time foregrounding its novelty and risk. This novelty and risk are inherent in undertaking something that Heidegger insists is untheorizable, that escapes the framework of any "attitude" [*Einstellung*], and that makes no appeal to familiar notions. Thus, what it actually means to "encounter" the gods is only graspable in the doing of it. All that Heidegger wants to put forth is a series of pointers to, and perhaps boundary markers of, a performance.

The central work in Heidegger's unpublished *oeuvre* from the "thirties" is without a doubt the *Contributions to Philosophy* (GA 65). This work launched a series of lengthy manuscripts, likewise unpublished by Heidegger, that occupy thousands of pages in the *Collected Edition*. My discussion in this section draws primarily upon just part of this vast corpus: Besides the *Contributions*, I rely chiefly on *Meditation* [*Besinnung*] (GA 66), *Metaphysics and Nihilism* (GA 67), as well as numerous shorter notes and sketches that have appeared collectively in volume 73 of the *Edition* (*Zum Ereignis-Denken*), itself close to 1500 pages long. Beginning with the *Contributions* one can see right away that Heidegger is concerned to explain the distinctiveness of his philosophical "saying" in the work ahead. The "philosophy" contained in the *Contributions*, and pursued relentlessly in the coming years, is not intended to be descriptive or explanative. Rather, it comprises a series of speech acts that "project" what Heidegger takes to be a radically new way of thinking. Heidegger's philosophical experiment has no precedent, it has no "clue [*Anhalt*]" to guide it, or else it would be mere "variation on the heretofore [*Abwandlung des Bisherigen*]" (GA 65, 4–6). Note the characteristically Heideggerian nominalization of the adjective "*bisherig*," meaning "previous," "former," and "up until now." The philosophical tradition is a has-been, like a dance routine that has become rote and uninspiring. Thus, what Heidegger is attempting is a creative "leap," the actual "performance [*Vollzug*]" of a genuinely new question (or line of questioning) (GA 65, 10–11). Nothing is being "proven" or "demonstrated" by the undertaking, including any answer to the question of why it is required in the first place. Heidegger's experiment in performative philosophy "has no ready-made place to stand [*Standplatz*]," and it cannot be evaluated or appraised according to the available normative schemes and conceptions of value (GA 65, 16–17).

In later notes, Heidegger likewise stresses the "irreplaceability" [*Unersetzbarkeit*] of the actual "performance" [*Vollzug*] of his experiment in thinking (GA 73.1, 153). This is because its results cannot be fully characterized ahead of time by means of any concept. To be understood, what Heidegger is saying must be undertaken. Here, too, Heidegger styles what is to be performed a "leap." He notes how, when a person leaps or jumps, a space is opened between them and the ground on which they formerly stood. This space, Heidegger maintains, must be "taken over" or "occupied" to be grasped, for it cannot be characterized externally, but "only in the *full-filment* [*volle Zug*]" (GA 73.1, 161). It requires a kind of intellectual courage to remain suspended in the "between" in this way. The "leap" involves a state of alienation or estrangement [*Ent-fremdung*] "from what is familiar and common – even in philosophy" (GA 73.1, 249). At the same time, it is "only through acting, through making an attempt [*Versuch*]" that what Heidegger is saying can be understood (GA 73.1, 279). In the "leap," one leaves behind the "heretofore," without arriving at a new position [*Stellung*]. To do philosophy this way, says Heidegger, entails "unleashing [*Anlassen*] the highest creative [*schaffend*] force – enabling [it] – liberating [it] – [and a] power for holding out – as a fundamental performance [*Grundvollzug*] of Da-*sein*" (GA 73.1, 332–333). As in his lecture course of 1920–1921 (see Section 1), Heidegger wants to differentiate between this "*knowing performance* [*Vollzug*] *of being*" and the stance of the observer, whose gaze washes out what is distinctive, and removes what is at stake in the matter (GA 73.1, 340, 333). Philosophy once again means enacting a Situation, adopting a style of being human, and articulating its otherwise hidden background conditions.

In the notes collected in GA73, Heidegger frequently revisits and revises prior directions in his thinking. In the 1920s, including in *Being and Time*, Heidegger (influentially) characterizes his philosophical approach as phenomenological *hermeneutics*, as the *interpretation* or rendering explicit of the concealed background conditions of life.[28] Now, in the "thirties," Heidegger undertakes a serious revision. "There is only interpretation where this is already a 'text,'" he observes, "*– but this has to now be written for the first time!*" (GA 73.1, 507, emphasis added). Nothing is being described, no typology or classification is being put forth (recall once more the argument in the 1920–1921 lectures), instead there is sheer "projection" of possibility (GA 73.1, 546). Neither explanatory causes nor transcendental conditions will be discovered. And, as Heidegger indicates many times in his writings from the "thirties," the motivation for this radical move is to be found in the "all or nothing" stakes of the situation we face in modern life. "It has been becoming clear for several decades now ... we face either a *total revolution* [*Gesamtumwälzung*] (performing [*vollziehen*] it – undertaking it), or *total confusion* [*Wirrnis*]. That's the decision" (GA 73.1, 552). It's time to go for broke philosophically.

GA82 is particularly valuable for clearly exhibiting Heidegger's experimental approach to philosophy, which involves continuous revision, rewriting, and reinterpretation of what he had already said. Many of the texts collected in this volume come from Heidegger's "thirties," and overlap in various ways with other writings from this period. Among other provocative claims, Heidegger says a number of times that *Being and Time* has been utterly misunderstood, for example, as transcendental philosophy. But *Being and Time* is properly comprehended "not as a description of conditions of possibility, but rather as a projecting, constructive leap into the ground of being human [*Menschsein*] as that which preserves the truth of historical being [*Seyn*]" (GA 82, 21). That is, *Being and Time* is an attempt to perform a *new way of being a human being*, not to describe the conditions of "everydayness." Again, this leap must be carried out "over against the Heretofore," and it must aim at "the performance [*Vollzug*] of a transformation [*Verwandlung*]," which includes the familiar frameworks for categorizing philosophical theories (GA 82, 23).

Being and Time, Heidegger now (ca. 1936) says, undertakes, or documents an attempt to undertake, a kind of ontological revision of what it means to be human. Dasein, the central topic or subject matter [*Sache*] of *Being and Time*, is not a natural kind but rather a gesture toward "the overcoming of being human, for the sake of new possibilities" (GA 82, 38). It is now clear to him, Heidegger says, that "Da-sein is not at all anything given – nor can it be *discovered* [*vor-zufinden*]. Being the *Da* has to be '*performed*' (created) – hence it is also unanalyzable" (GA 82, 38). This might not have been obvious to people, Heidegger suggests, because of what calls the "*phenomenological illusion* [*Täuschung*]." This illusion is the

---

[28] See Crowe 2019.

semblance that "Da-sein is being described and analyzed here like something present at hand" (GA 82, 45). The phenomenological illusion makes it seem as though what Heidegger is trying to construct in *Being and Time* is a *better description* of what it is to be human, but "what it all comes down to is the leap, and the transformation of the essence of truth!" (GA 82, 58).

It is no easy matter to get a handle on what Heidegger is saying about his approach to philosophy in these texts. It is clear enough what philosophy is *not* supposed to be. It is neither description nor analysis nor classification nor explanation nor transcendental argumentation. It is a performative transformation of being human that cannot be made intelligible in terms of the familiar options. At the same time, the philosophical performance evinces its own structure, as if a play were being written by the actors on the stage as they interacted with each other. Consider a familiar example, such as Shakespeare's *Julius Caesar*. In the standard, non-Heideggerian version of the play, who the characters are, what it is that they are going to turn out to do, and the ultimate result of their actions are knowable prior to the performance of the play. Of course, part of the joy of theater is that there is no deterministic relationship between the playwright's script and how a particular actor chooses to portray a character. But it's clear enough that who Mark Antony is in *Julius Caesar* is largely determined by what Shakespeare has him say, do, and undergo in the play. Moreover, the writer, the actors, and the audience can all draw upon a shared fund of ordinary concepts and background information that make it possible for the play to actually communicate something.

But suppose that *Julius Caesar* were in fact a Heideggerian play, a play without any text, that makes no reference to a shared fund of beliefs and concepts. Who Mark Antony is in this version of *Julius Caesar* is indeterminate so long as the play is being performed. It's not even obvious that this version would need to have Mark Antony in it at all, for Mark Antony's role in the events around Julius Caesar's death is something we expect to find in the play because we have preexisting beliefs about how things went. Shakespeare, we can say, knew that he needed to have Mark Antony in there somewhere, or else no one would buy his version of *Julius Caesar* as a historical drama. In a Heideggerian version of *Julius Caesar*, however, we should have no expectations about what will be portrayed. Even the title, *Julius Caesar*, will function not to reference a familiar personage from history but rather to indicate or point us toward a performance called "being Julius Caesar" with no preexisting script, that dispenses with any and all expectations about what a play called *Julius Caesar* is going to be about. Everything that we believed previously about what plays involve is held in suspense. Supposing that this analogy fits what Heidegger says he is doing in texts like *Contributions to Philosophy*, it starts to become difficult to discern a motivation for taking up his project. And there is no suggestion from Heidegger about how someone might know whether or not it had been worth it to make the "leap."

It is important to keep in mind Heidegger's adoption of this radically performative approach to philosophy while considering what he says about God, the gods, and religion. What he is doing with enigmatic gestures toward "the last god," for example, is indicating a risk-filled, unscripted *performance* of the basic relationship between humanity and the divine. We cannot be sure that either humanity *or* the divine will be met with in the leap, rather than "refused." Heidegger is not trying to describe what religion is, or to demonstrate either its truth or falsehood. Instead, by dismantling metaphysics, Heidegger hopes, at least in part, to clear the ground for "leaping" into a relationship that is not defined ahead of time in any precise way. There is no way to be sure about what the "leap" will yield, and if we try to achieve such security ahead of time we will have rendered it impossible to undertake by means of lingering entanglements in metaphysics. Recall how, in 1920–1921, Heidegger had set forth remarkable insights into what it would mean to perform or undertake a life that issues from a radical *reversal* of values. Paul and his churches could be said to be undertaking a new possibility of being religious that begins with a profound rupture with all that came before. Heidegger, too, initiates a rupture with "the Heretofore" for the sake of a "new inception," which he styles in the *Contributions* as a "liberation" (GA 65, 10). This is nothing less than a *Wesenswandel*, a transformation of the essence of what it is to be human (GA 65, 3, 16–17). Moreover, Heidegger says, it is only by means of such a transformation that, "fitting into the joint [*fügend in die Fuge*] of historical being [*Seyn*], we stand at the disposal of [*Verfügung*] the gods," who are "the most distant ones" (GA 65, 18). Put simply, one thing Heidegger is doing in the *Contributions* and related works is giving a "pointer [*Weisung*]" to a transformation of the relations that constitute what things *are* for us, what they mean, which is itself a matter of what they are *to each other*. The "new inception" involves configuring a new joint or junction [*Fuge*] of possibilities of meaning in which a new "divinizing" [*Götterung*] of God or the gods can take place (GA 65, 4). What Heidegger seems to be saying is that what it is to be divine, along with what it is to be human, must be transformed through a "leap" into a new way of enacting new, unforeseeable dimensions of meaning.

2.2 God and Metaphysics

As already mentioned, the entanglement of God and metaphysics is one of Heidegger's lifelong philosophical concerns. In Section 3, I will describe one of the ways this concern appears after Heidegger's "thirties," in the postwar years.

In this section, I will investigate one line of thought present in Heidegger's writings from his "thirties," writings that can be seen as the workshop, the proverbial shed out back, where Heidegger tinkered and ultimately assembled the central components of his later philosophy. For this very reason, these texts often display a strenuous and sometimes provocative clarity, while preserving the sense of creative risk and exploration that attends Heidegger's project. The picture Heidegger presents here is roughly the following. With Plato and Aristotle, the question about what things are becomes the question of what *grounds* or *explains* what there is. The basic schema under which God is subsequently understood is the concept of such an ultimate explanatory ground. In something like the way "pagan" deities are seen as deifications of natural and social powers by critical Church Fathers, the metaphysical conception of God is viewed by Heidegger as a "deification" of this idea of a cause. Heidegger further maintains that it is this very fact about the metaphysical conception of God that enabled the reversal of this process of deification in modernity with the death of God. The original direction of explanation, from God to things as a whole, is turned around when something else – namely, subjectivity, reason, and will – becomes the ground. Aristotle as it were sets it up for Nietzsche.[29]

At an early point in the *Contributions* Heidegger suggests what is important about understanding this metaphysical schematization, as well as about moving past it. The "divine," whatever it may be, is whatever "surpasses" [*übersteigen*]. But all of the available ways of conceptualizing this presuppose a rigid or fixed determination of that which is being "surpassed" (GA 65, 24–25). In this way, the relation between the divine and the human likewise becomes fixed, while what needs to happen is for all of this to be "dislodged" [*verrückt*] (GA 65, 25). This is roughly similar to what Heidegger had said in 1920–1921, namely, that a conception of scientific knowledge as objective (as taking up a distinctive "attitude" [*Einstellung*]) makes it impossible to appreciate what Paul and the early Christians are actually doing, i.e., relating to God in a radically different way. There are, however, at least two differences between these accounts. First, in the *Contributions* and related texts, it is not just a conception of knowledge, but *Western philosophy* or metaphysics per se, that applies a rigid framework to the relationship between the divine and the human. Second, Heidegger is no longer investigating a specifically Christian kind of religiosity. Instead, what

---

[29] This is how Heidegger explains things as well in 1940 lectures on Nietzsche, where Descartes and Kant are singled out as being particularly significant in this process of reversal (GA 48, 305–309). I am tempted to call this move *reductio ad Fredericanum*. Heidegger's interpretation of Nietzsche and of Nietzsche's position in the history of metaphysics, and the related engagement with Ernst Jünger, would be an apt subject of a separate Element in this series. As such I will leave my own questions about these matters to the side.

Heidegger is getting at is that there is something about the way the divine–human relation has been configured metaphysically, in terms of "surpassing," "transcendence," and, ultimately, in terms of power, that Heidegger thinks has reached its terminal stage.

A clear and direct statement of Heidegger's general picture of metaphysics comes from 1941 lectures on Schelling (titled "The Metaphysics of German Idealism"). Heidegger writes: "Since Plato and Aristotle the question about the *on* [that which is], i.e., about its *archai* [principles] and *aitia* [causes], [is] the question about the *theion* [the divine], and thus *prote philosophie episteme theologike* [first philosophy is theological science], thence Christianity's variations (GA 49, 111)."[30]

Here, in the classroom context, Heidegger declares what he also elaborates in more detail in private writings. For example, in § 18 of *Meditation*, the next in the series of unpublished works following the *Contributions to Philosophy*, Heidegger explains how the question about the ground of what there is can receive a theological answer when the divine is understood as what is "highest" or "supreme" (GA 66, 231). The next step is for the divine to become "reified" [*dinghafte*] and given an explanative function as "creator."[31] "God" refers henceforth to "the unconditioned, infinite ground of beingness and the cause of beings" (GA 66, 242). For Heidegger, this was a fateful maneuver. "[E]verything in Western history up till now," he says, flows from taking the divine as "a being," even when God is styled "being itself" [*das Sein selbst*] (GA 66, 255–256). The primary mover of the entire metaphysical tradition is the quest for "explanation" [*Erklärung*], which, Heidegger says at one point, is simultaneously a process of "idealization" or "apotheosis" [*Verklärung*]. That is, whatever the ultimate *explanans* might happen to be, it is elevated to a distinctive status of *supremacy*. The most fundamental is also the highest.

Heidegger takes it that all such objects of "deification" eventually lose their divinity. In precisely this way, the God of metaphysics comes to be seen (by Nietzsche) as "the cause or object of a drive," that which is merely "superhuman" in the sense of being a projection of human deficiency (GA 66, 241). This de- or un-deifying [*Entgötterung*] is the inevitable result of the initial deification

---

[30] I have transliterated the Greek and provided common, i.e., non-Heideggerian, translations in brackets here. Heidegger's text uses the Greek letters and does not include any translations.

[31] In notes related to Hegel from the early 1940s, we read more about this process of explanatory ascent: "The distinction between beings and beingness posits the latter (beingness) as the condition – unconditioned and *therefore* [*deshalb*] higher, and as a being that is, the supreme [*Seiendste*] – the *primal* thing [*Ur-sache*]. A gradation [*Stufung*] from lower to higher is already marked off in this distinction – this gradation finds multiple forms, each one according to the relation of beingness (*idea* and *idein*) – i.e., according to the level of knowledge as the guiding relation to beings" (GA 86, 308).

[*Vergötterung*]. What has been missed, he says, is that while other gods are polemically cast as mere deifications of specific natural or social forces, the "Christian-Jewish God is not the deification of a particular cause of some effect, but rather of what it is to be a cause [*Ursachsein*] as such, of whatever is represented to be explanative as such" (GA 66, 239–240). Seen in this light, the allegedly higher "spirituality" of the monotheistic conception of God vis-à-vis the lesser deities of the "pagans" is really only a "semblance" that is grounded not on God per se but on the concept of "causality as such" (GA 66, 240).[32]

Elsewhere, Heidegger tries out a different versions of this historical narrative (e.g., GA 73.1, 819, 823, 996; GA 48, 300–302). The details are seemingly less important to Heidegger than the acknowledgment that mistake is being made when God is schematized according to metaphysics. It is "always worthwhile," he says in other notes, "to ask whether the claim that God is the supreme being [*Seiendste*] among beings says something divine about God" (GA 73.1, 991). In another unpublished manuscript on metaphysics, Heidegger maintains that all metaphysical concepts are in fact "ground-concepts" [*Grundbegriffe*], or "*arche*-concepts," and briefly discusses classical metaphysical terms like *arche*, *aition, causa, principium*, and "condition of possibility" (GA 67, 55). Here the idea is that metaphysics involves a regress to what is meant to be ultimately explanatory (GA 67, 24). Heidegger likewise describes how beingness [*Seiendheit*] comes to be ascribed to or identified with the "supreme being" [*Seiendste*], as in the Thomistic formula *deus est ipsum esse*. This connection makes all metaphysics theological, in the sense that it "derives beings from a supreme being as first cause."[33] This just means, Heidegger says, that God has in fact been "delivered over to calculating and explaining" (GA 67, 94).

What is it that Heidegger finds so problematic about the metaphysical conception of God? For one thing, it is clear to him that the notion of a "first cause," or "highest being," of the beingness of beings gets in the way of seeing the deeper background conditions of intelligibility that he calls "historical being" [*Seyn*].[34] But, with respect to thinking about God specifically, it would seem that

---

[32] Several sections of the 1941 "continuation [*Fortsetzung*]" of the earlier manuscript, *Überwindung der Metaphysik*, echo this analysis of the relation between metaphysics and theology. In § 87, Heidegger argues that the concept of the transcendental Ideal (in the *Critique of Pure Reason*) aligns Kant's philosophical theology with metaphysics (GA 67, 92). In § 90, he summarizes the picture as presented in the lectures on Schelling and in *Besinnung* (GA 67, 94). § 92 is discussed later in this section.

[33] Heidegger elsewhere outlines the primary concepts in such theologized metaphysics. "Beings" [*das Seiende*] are conceived as *totum ens creatum* (*finitum*) [the totality of created (finite) being], while "being" [*das Sein*] is *ens creator* [creator being] – *deus est suum esse* [God is His being], God is "infinite" being, the "highest" [*akrotaton*] being (GA 73.2, 1093).

[34] In one place, Heidegger refers to this as the "nihilism of Christianity," or "the fact that it employs thinking as *believing* [*Glauben*], butting in between and elevating itself above itself and thus – as excess [*Überstieg*] – *holding back* everything in half measures and delaying everything – every

metaphysics involves the following. What it means for things to be is, simply, for them to be created, produced, or brought forth [*Her-gestelltes*], and so made present. This causal or productive understanding of beings does not mandate that any particular being has to be the fundamental cause, as long as there is one; hence, because metaphysics as it were "promoted" God to this place, God can very well be "demoted" later on when a different way of explaining what there is achieves its ascendency. The rigid schema of ground–consequent, cause–effect, and agent–patient is what is actually fundamental to metaphysics, not any particular notion of God per se. Instead, Heidegger's point is that what (or who) God is becomes fixed or defined within this explanatory regress. It need not be God that plays the explanatory function, and indeed God can be just as easily one of the *explananda*, while the relation stays the same in a formal or abstract sense. From a metaphysical perspective, *something or other* has to be "supreme," "surpassing," "transcendent," meaning that something has to have the primary causal power that completes the explanatory regress.

2.3 Neediness

Having seen what it is that Heidegger is aiming to dismantle or overcome, the next step is to try to understand what he says about the possibilities that this maneuver opens up. To summarize some very complicated and elusive prose, Heidegger points to the thought that both the divine – God, the gods, the last god – and human beings "need" historical being [*Seyn*], and the way it "fits" or "joins" [*fügen*] things together in relations of meaning. This, in turn, suggests a relationship of reciprocity or mutuality, in which each of the *relata* is indispensable to the other and neither has priority or supremacy. Viewed in the context of historical being [*Seyn*], what joins the divine and the human (if at all) is no longer the causal power of one or the other. God and humanity escape the schema of metaphysics. The precise nature of the relationship is left wholly indeterminate by Heidegger, but it is clear that it involves a serious reconfiguration of the standard relations of priority. One of the many intriguing possibilities for thinking further along Heidegger's lines here is to reconsider the fundamental relatedness of God within the context of Biblical religion. That is, Heidegger is opening up a possibility for understanding Biblical language about God in a nondoctrinal and non-metaphysical way (see Section 2.4).

As discussed Section 2.2, Heidegger calls for a way of thinking that serves to dislodge the thinker and what is being thought about from the framework of metaphysics. When this happens, thought unfolds in the uncertain domain

---

possibility of *twisting free* [*Verwindung*] – i.e., [every possibility of] the experience of historical being [*Seyn*]!" (GA 73.2, 1126).

[*Bereich*] of the "between," in which, to be sure, "the gods remain in flight," but within which any possibilities for relationship to the divine must be disclosed. A "fissure" or "rift" [*Zerklüftung*] must be opened, making a space that "in first grounding itself sets apart gods and human beings and turns them to face one another" (GA 65, 28–29). We must abandon "the crutch of the 'why?'," he says, and undertake a "leap" (GA 65, 19). According to Heidegger, the "between" requires from us a stance of "restraint [*Verhaltenheit*]" or reticence that leaves the relation between gods and human beings indeterminate. These points help to exclude certain interpretations of what Heidegger means when, later on in the *Contributions* he ponders the mysterious figure of the "last god." Heidegger is not to be understood there as asserting a metaphysical thesis, e.g., that there is (or was?) a divine being who comes "last" (in a series of them?). Nor is Heidegger proclaiming "deliverance" or salvation for humanity with some new "revelation" (GA 65, 327). Nor is he setting forth a normative claim, for example by trying to establish a "worldview" or a hierarchy of values (GA 65, 36–41). What Heidegger is doing is experimenting with a way of thinking about the divine that has no reference to what people have hitherto and for the most part taken that to involve.

Lest readers imagine that Heidegger is asserting some historical sequence of divine dispensations, he explains that "last," in "the last god," does not refer to "sheer stoppage and ending" (GA 65, 324–325). Being last in the way the "last god" is "last" signifies *extremity*, standing at the limit of what can be thought or said about the divine, or perhaps beyond the limit of what can be said or thought. What is furthest out or most extreme in this sense is simultaneously a different "inception of the immeasurable possibilities of our history" (GA 65, 326). The extremities point beyond themselves to something unthought. Alternatively, to speak of the "last god" is to speak of what there is left to say or think about God at this moment of extremity in Western history. Again, what is important to Heidegger is that the "last god" is not the *final* one, not a hard limit or barrier, but more like a narrow doorway that we can squeeze through in order to get to the other side. The extremity of the last god also calls to mind its incalculability, the fact that the last god does not fall into any of the familiar categories of metaphysical or theological positions. "The last god," Heidegger says, "has its own most unique uniqueness, and stands outside the calculative determination expressed in the labels 'mono-theism,' 'pan-theism,' 'a-theism'" (GA 65, 325). That is to say, God, in the sense of *summum ens* of metaphysics, is not being named or thought of at all. The last god belongs to "what is unable to be thought in advance" (GA 65, 329). The last god is in motion, it passes by or is passing by. Such a god is not simply present or available, but rather, in a sense, insubstantial, and so is quite unsuitable as the ultimate explanatory ground of beings as a whole. Someone who is just "passing by" is itinerant, untethered, here-today-gone-tomorrow. Later on in this section and the following one, I'll suggest how this configuration of the "last god" overlaps with the way God is portrayed (as present and absent) in the scriptures of Judaism and Christianity.

In the figure of the last god, Heidegger is gesturing at the possibility that the divine "needs historical being [*Seyn*]," which somehow does not mean that the god "renounces itself or its greatness" (GA 65, 327). The neediness of the god is not a diminishment, since the relation between historical being [*Seyn*] and the god is not causal, does not involve power.[35] Human beings "belong" to historical being [*Seyn*] in a different way, and yet do so "through the god." Human beings "need" the god in order to belong to historical being [*Seyn*], Heidegger says. What does he mean by this? In what sense of "through" do human beings belong, via the god, to historical being [*Seyn*]? Heidegger does not elaborate much in these paragraphs. A general picture does suggest itself, however. Both the god and humanity need a space that makes possible or enables relations between them. Without finding a place in such a space, the god is simply the "beyond," that which is utterly unintelligible for being outside any conceivable relationship with human beings. For their part, human beings, who hold open the "between," need to be dislodged, as it were, from being blindly involved with what immediately concerns them. The god in its extremity draws human beings out of themselves in an effort to come to terms with what is almost (but not quite) totally beyond their ken. The humans need the god or the gods to *be human*, and the former need historical being [*Seyn*] in order to be disclosed to the latter.[36]

In Heidegger's 1941 lectures on Schelling, he likewise points to the indispensability of the background or "space" in which things are first "able to be placed [*setzbar*]" (GA 49, 61). Attending to this space requires renunciation or "divestment" [*Entäußerung*] from "the primacy of *any* being [*Vorherrschaft irgeneins Seienden*], even of the former [*bisherigen*] God, over being" (GA 49, 63). In other words, Heidegger is once again saying that we have to divest from metaphysics in order to appreciate the more original possibilities. Because of what it requires, such an appreciation is, again, a "leap" that has scarcely been previously intimated (GA 65, 69). According to Heidegger, despite the originality of his approach in the *Freiheitsschrift* of 1809 (the most important text in Schelling's corpus for Heidegger), Schelling is still involved in an explanatory project, in seeking a "demonstration [*Nachweisung*] of beings in the ether of the

---

[35] Heidegger reflects on this point in an undated note, stressing that "need" here does not imply "deficiency" or "lack" (GA 73.2, 992).

[36] Heidegger makes the same point, I take it, though more poetically, elsewhere, writing of how the gods "light a fire" that is mirrored in the *Gegenblick* [returned glance?] of the human "hearth fire" (GA 73.1, 823–824).

absolute" (GA 49, 119). That is, Schelling is still doing metaphysics. At the same time, or perhaps despite himself, Schelling does anticipate Heidegger by grasping the way in which God *needs* beings in order to be manifest or revealed. Heidegger captures Schelling's key point this way: "God can only see *himself* as existing in *something independent of him*" (GA 65, 128). Despite the proximity of this thought to what Heidegger is exploring in texts from his "thirties," it is clear that this is not what Heidegger has in mind. Heidegger is not saying that God or the gods "need" beings, but rather that they need historical being [*Seyn*]. Furthermore, Schelling's conception of divine creation as self-expression or self-externalization is not part of the line of thought Heidegger is pursuing.

Heidegger's most extended discussion of the ideas about God first broached in the *Contributions* comes in GA 66, a lengthy unpublished manuscript called *Meditation*. At the start of a segment of the text devoted to the topic, Heidegger calls attention to the fact that, in the late modern era, "gods have become impossible: Their flight has been decided in this age" (GA 66, 237). Indeed, the absence of the gods is what gives the present age its distinctive "stamp" [*Gepräge*], a thought Heidegger drew from his reading of Hölderlin and Nietzsche (GA 66, 237). Heidegger demands that the situation be confronted with steadfastness, which means that recourse should not be had to the schema of metaphysics, nor should any certainty be sought (GA 66, 229). We must allow ourselves to be sucked into the "whirlwind" [*Wirbelstürme*] of history, staking our very "essence" as human beings (at least as understood up to this point) (GA 66, 238). Staying true to this approach means that all Heidegger can do is offer a "pointer" or "indication" [*Hinweisung*] of the domain in which "the gods can be named, forgotten, or recollected" (GA 66, 229). Here, Heidegger envisions three ways that things might go should his pointer be taken up. Perhaps there will be a new inception, a new "establishment [*Stiftung*] of being." It is more realistic, however, to think that beings will linger on in the "shackles" of the "tangled up, mixed up" framework of metaphysics in a way that excludes the possibility of any real decision and simply carries on with the same old thing. Or, just maybe, while this framework might linger, something different might happen in the "heart space [*Herzenraum*]" of the rare and the few (GA 66, 230–231).

The key point is that Heidegger's pointer leads away from conceptualizing the gods "as the highest in the sense of metaphysical thinking and poetic creation up till now," and this means coming to appreciate them as "belonging to the neediness [*Notschaft*] of historical being [*Seyn*] that pervades [*durchschwingt*] everything" (GA 66, 231).[37] Heidegger writes: "Gods do not create

---

[37] Heidegger adds a further layer to the relation between the gods and "historical being" in a difficult passage of notes: "The God, who is as the highest being, needs historical being. But historical being is never able to causally bring God about. Historical being is not able to bring

human beings, nor do human beings discover gods. The truth of historical being [*Seyn*] decides 'about' both, not by holding power over them, but rather by first adapting itself [*ereignet sich*] between them, and so first becoming apt for *encounter* [*Ent-gegnung*] (GA 66, 235)."

The term Heidegger uses – *Entgegnung* – for the relation between gods and human beings that he is trying to indicate obviously requires some explication. *Gegnen* is a verbal form derived from a preposition, *gegen*, meaning "against," "opposed to," or *contra*, and it only appears in combination with prefixes such as in the case of *entgegnen*. The latter has two connotations that are important for Heidegger's usage. First, "*entgegnen*" has the sense of meeting with something or being met with something, comparable to Latin *occurrare*. At the same time, it also has the sense of responding, replying, or answering back. In the passage just quoted, Heidegger draws attention to the prefix *ent-*; in an *Ent-gegnung*, the contrariety or opposition is removed, taken away, or reversed. The English word "encounter," though it has a different derivation, captures something of the inherent tension Heidegger is highlighting, likewise suggesting movement in opposite directions being suspended or reversed. The English word comes from two Latin prepositions, *in* and *contra*, and calls to mind two things coming to face one another contrariwise and establishing some relation between themselves. It is important to see that, in an "encounter," the movement is not unidirectional. By contrast, in the framework of metaphysics as Heidegger understands it, one being is the cause or ground of the other, and hence "higher" than the other.[38]

While Heidegger does not envision a power differential in his idea of the "encounter" of gods and humanity, it is plain that he is also trying to preserve or capture a normative dimension to this relation. In the encounter, the gods can be said to "compel" or "necessitate" [*ernötigen*] human beings to "take over" the task of "custodianship" [*Wächterschaft*] of the "between" in which the encounter takes place. The "between" is the *Da*, the open space, both "here" and "there," which is the condition of all meaningful interaction (GA 66, 242). Something like a *claim* is put upon humanity by the gods, who "need" historical being [*Seyn*], and so "need" human beings to take the latter into custody. This encounter is not yet or no longer "religion," which is merely "sinking back into some form of deifying beings" (GA 66, 243). For this reason, Heidegger's talk of the gods is not intended to satisfy "religious needs" in an age in which

---

God into unconcealedness before and from itself. The God, if He is the God, must arrive [*ankomme*] on his own into the historical being that He needs." "This need is no deficiency. The more present something present is, the more decisively and unrestrictedly it needs appropriation [*Ereignis*]" (GA 73.2, 992).

[38] Heidegger discusses similar ideas in an undated note regarding not *Entgegnung* but *Vergegnung*, which usually means "mishap" or "misencounter," but which he wants to reconfigure as an initial lack of fit that is creative, an original way of sharing a "neighborhood [*Gegend*]" (GA 73.1, 781–782).

institutional forms of religion have declined in prestige and influence in people's lives (GA 66, 248–249). Indeed, no particular or determinate idea of what it is to be divine is being assumed here. The term "god," rather, "names only the empty place of the indeterminacy of divinity." Heidegger makes no claim to "certainty about a 'being [*Wesen*]' that is present some place and active some way" (GA 66, 249). Nor does he think we should opt for private "faithfulness" [*Gläubigkeit*] somehow outside of any institutional framework. What he is suggesting is a move that is much thinner, much more attenuated and noncommittal than these excluded possibilities, but which is that the same time highly risky, a question of who we are as human beings at the deepest level.

For these reasons, there is something ill-fitting about the term "religion" for the topic of Heidegger's reflections in these texts. The unmooring from metaphysics that is required for the "leap" involves holding in suspense concepts that are familiar. Heidegger draws attention to the problematic of "religion" in this passage:

> Only in the domain of metaphysics, and in its essential variants, is the relation to "God" something "religious" – a *religio*, a binding back to a first cause and controlling. The concept of *religio* is meta-physical, i.e., it arises out of how beings are tied back to and established upon a highest being – the "supreme being" [*Seiendste*], because it is causative [*Verursachende*]. Both formerly and today this "highest" being is called "being," [for example] in "existential philosophy." (GA 67, 95)

Following these observations, Heidegger reprises his account of the fusion of theology and metaphysics, or of the metaphysical schematization of God (GA 67, 95). What he is calling attention to in the quoted passage is that there is a relation of causal power at the basis of "religion." "Religion," he suggests, is an attempt to gain power, control, security, by establishing a relationship with the ultimate or original power. This means that talk of Heidegger and "religion" has to be cautiously undertaken. The "leap" into something more original than "religion" can only be indicated or pointed to with such familiar designations. There is, in fact, something "godless" about what Heidegger is intimating, in the sense that what has typically be thought of as "god" is not part of the picture (see Section 3). Some later notes set this forth in austere, hyphenated lines: "Without god-hood [*Gott-heit*]. Without the gods and without God" (GA 73.1, 822). Heidegger says that the "without [*ohne*]" in the above does not connote a merely negative relation to "what was possessed formerly [*vorigen Habe*]," in particular "'being' as *ens entium* (cf. [Aristotle's] *Metaphysics* Book XI.9, *timiotaton on* [most honored being])." Nor does "godlessness" here connote "free thinking" or the "*substitute ideas* [*Ersatzige-bilde*] that surface in its wake" (GA 73.1, 823).[39] Instead, what Heidegger is indicating is a lack of determinacy or decision that can only be clarified by performing the "leap."

2.4 Reading God Non-metaphysically

At the beginning of this section, I argued that, while not all of what Heidegger offers needs to be accepted, there are nonetheless valuable possibilities that his revolutionary philosophical *intinerarium* unearths. It will be recalled that I likened the "leap" called for by Heidegger to something more like a "plunge." Heidegger himself observes that he is not "interpreting" anything, since interpretation requires there be a "text" that has already been composed and is waiting to be read. Heidegger's radical experiment is necessarily "godless," meaning that it happens independently of any previous commitments about what it will uncover, which may or may not involve God. Indeed, Heidegger's oscillation between different terms, "God," "the god," "the gods," "the last god," is meant precisely to capture the conceptual indeterminacy involved in the undertaking. I also argued previously that Heidegger does not convincingly motivate the necessity of this experiment, in that his conception of the "plight" or "emergency" [*Not*] of modernity is itself questionable. If I am right about that, if there is indeed reason to resist something about Heidegger's picture of the intellectual landscape, then nothing requires that any and all "texts" – things to think about – be cast aside as part of the "heretofore." What can be more readily accepted from Heidegger is that there is a certain framework of concepts called "metaphysics" that should not necessarily be assumed or taken for granted as the proper basis for understanding God. Heidegger had tried to rescind from the objectifying attitude implied by the canonical view of "scientific" philosophy in 1920–1921; his writings from the "thirties" recommend that the same be done with metaphysics. Holding this framework in suspense surely does not require rejecting "the heretofore" in its entirety, in the way Heidegger would seem to suggest. To reflect back on what Heidegger does in 1920–1921, it is more reasonable to think that pursuing a phenomenology of religion entails no claim that one should not ever try to understand religion scientifically. If it did, it would be unreasonable to pursue phenomenology. Heidegger's own procedure shows how the phenomenological project incorporates concepts and results of other approaches, especially as launching points for its own investigations (e.g., critical New Testament scholarship). Similarly, trying to think about the relation between God and humanity

---

[39] Heidegger elsewhere emphasizes that, while his attempt to think historical being [*Seyn*] is totally distinct from "calling upon [*rufen*] God," the two activities are for that very reason not opposed or in conflict (GA 73.2, 994).

non-metaphysically entails no claim that thinking about these things metaphysically is always an error. No arguments from Heidegger are forthcoming that support such a conclusion, whatever he himself may have thought about the matter. If thinking non-metaphysically excludes every other way of thinking, then it is not reasonable to think non-metaphysically. Heidegger *assumes* that extreme measures are called for by extremity; he does not show that it is so.

Thinking non-metaphysically, like all thinking, needs something to think about.[40] This holds for thinking about God. To start thinking non-metaphysically about God there must be a way of specifying what we are going to be thinking about. It would not do, of course, to borrow what is being thought about directly or indirectly from metaphysics. Fortunately, as Heidegger recognizes, there is a different way of specifying what it is that we are thinking about when we think about God non-metaphysically. "God," in addition to being the term for a metaphysical concept, is also the name for a character in a story, a *person*. I am thinking, of course, about the way God is characterized throughout the Bible (inclusive of Jewish and Christian scripture, with the former referred to henceforth as Jewish Bible/O[ld]T[estament]). Thinking non-metaphysically about God could mean trying to decipher this character while holding in suspense doctrinal and metaphysical commitments.

If one takes up the Bible, especially the Jewish scriptures known to Christians as the Old Testament (OT), in a non-metaphysical way, that means the focus is no longer on what God needs to be like in order to be the absolute, unconditioned, first cause, the being that stops the regress of metaphysical explanation. One potential outcome of such an approach is that what are traditionally known as God's "attributes" or "perfections" are not any longer straightforwardly derivative of God's function as *ens creator*. As has been observed many times in debates about theism, the concept of an intelligible or supernatural cause must itself be consistent, i.e., possible, or else there is no question of its existing or explaining anything. But, if we follow up on Heidegger's suggestion and suspend the metaphysical framework, then, once again, we need not be concerned with the question of what God needs to be in order to be an intelligible cause. Aspects of how God is portrayed in the Jewish Bible/OT seem to conflict with the conceptual requirements of being the first cause of all things. This is not to deny that there are ways of reading the text that reveal something more behind the surface layer of contradiction. What following up on Heidegger means in this case is reading the text of the Jewish Bible/OT without trying to overcome the tensions and apparent contradictions.

---

[40] For an alternative approach to the implications of Heidegger's criticisms of metaphysics for religion, see Wrathall and Lambeth 2011.

Heidegger is not to be read as substituting a new framework for "religion" in place of the old metaphysical one. Yet, in writings considered so far in this section, he does point to the possibility of reconceiving relations of priority as relations of reciprocity, and of emphasizing the relationality of things more generally. When approached non-metaphysically, the Jewish Bible/OT testifies abundantly to ways of thinking about God relationally. On Heidegger's picture, "the gods" and humanity do not simply mirror one another or reduce to one another. Their relation is many-sided or multidimensional in so far as both "depend" upon historical being [*Seyn*] to be fit or adapted [*geeignet*] to one another. Neither does God reduce to His relations with humanity in the Jewish Bible/OT. There is something opaque, independent, even inaccessible about who God is. Like the "last god," God is in motion, "passing by," never simply available. This is testified to in the texts in multiple ways. Crucially, God and humanity stand in a kind of mutuality that does not preclude independence. They are neither simply present nor simply absent to one another.[41]

In the Jewish Bible/OT, God is *holy*, meaning that the encounter with God must be set apart, protected, cordoned off. Holiness indicates irreducibility, as well as opacity. In one emblematic text, Leviticus 11, a list of things that render a person "unclean" is followed by this divine pronouncement: For I am the Lord your God; sanctify yourselves therefore, and be holy, for I am holy. You shall not defile yourselves with any swarming creature that moves on the earth. For I am the Lord who brought you up from the land of Egypt, to be your God; you shall be holy, for I am holy (Lev. 11:44–45)."

The concerns in Leviticus 11 are obviously cultic, having to do with what is required to maintain the beneficent presence of God among the people of Israel. God is not something commonplace, but something utterly set aside from all else. At the same time, *and in the very same passage*, God is not merely absent from the everyday, but is *related* to the people within historical reality. God is both holy *and* "your God." And yet, "the Lord your God is a devouring fire, a jealous God" (Deut. 4:24), and "who is there of all flesh that has heard the voice of the living God speaking out of fire, as we have, and remained alive?" (Deut. 5:26). In the great scene of the renewal of the covenant in the final chapter of Joshua, the title character declares to the people: "You cannot serve the Lord, for he is a holy God. He is a jealous God; he will not forgive your

---

[41] Modern classics of Biblical theology align with this Heideggerian conception to the extent that relation becomes the primary category for understanding what the Jewish Bible/OT says about God. The paradigm for this approach is Eichrodt 1961 and 1967. A more recent contributor is Walter Brueggemann. See especially Brueggemann 1997. A number of the Biblical passages I call upon here were first brought to my attention in connection with this topic by Brueggemann's book.

transgressions or your sins. If you forsake the LORD and serve foreign gods, then he will turn and do you harm, and consume you, after having done you good (Joshua 24:19–20)."

Ezekiel 16 picks up on this thread, giving a remarkable and searing recounting of a relationship gone awry, and the destructive jealousy that follows. This passage holds together poignant imagery of Israel as an abandoned child, cared for by God and elevated to the status of a beloved spouse, with a shocking denunciation of "lewdness" and "whoring," and a terrifying depiction of humiliation, sexual violence, and destruction. Once again, the Jewish Bible/OT is unconcerned with any merely logical or conceptual difficulty in its portrayal of God. The God who is unapproachable, wrathful, jealous, and destructive is *the very one* who loves Israel like a devoted husband. Psalm 22, known to Christians from the Good Friday liturgy, goes beyond even destructive fury to exhibit what it is to be abandoned by God, what it is for God to be simply *absent*. "Why are you so far from helping me, from the words of my groaning?" (Ps. 22:1). And yet, the Psalmist acknowledges amidst this anguish that "it was you who took me from the womb; you kept me safe on my mother's breast" (v. 9).

In his unpublished writings from the "thirties," Heidegger gestures at the possibility of mutuality or reciprocity between human beings and the divine. In the Jewish Bible/OT, it is not just human beings who are dependent upon God, or who suffer the consequences of a broken relationship. Who God is, and who Israel is, are both partly determined by their relationship. This is, of course, what the central concept of "covenant" involves. Who God is concretely comes down to his *promise* to be Israel's God, and who Israel is comes down to their promise to be his people. Numerous texts in the Jewish Bible/OT suggest a solemn liturgical reenactment of the founding of this relationship. Such acts of promising set up distinctive kinds of relationships. A promise projects or creates a future that is not simply the outcome of a sequence of events that would have transpired anyway. A promise likewise commits someone – in this case, God – to something. At the same time, God's promise in this instance founds human life not on something *present* and securely available, but rather on something that is *yet to come*, and thus unfulfilled. Both of the parties that are related by the promise are who they are not because of their present reality but rather because of *who they will turn out to have been* in the specific context of the relationship. Neither God nor human beings nor the nature of their relationship is identical to what it happens to be at the present time. Having made the promise, God has staked his *name*, as well as his *glory*. His name is profaned when Israel suffers and stumbles (Ezek. 39:7). This is reversed only when God recalls his promise and publicly demonstrates his loyalty to it. "Therefore thus says the Lord GOD: Now I will restore the fortunes of Jacob, and have mercy on the whole house of Israel; and I will be jealous for my holy name" (Ezek. 39:25).

When, following Heidegger's hints, the framework of metaphysics is suspended, it is possible to appreciate something of the distinctive creativity of the biblical portrayal of God. When we're no longer worried about whether or not God fits into an explanatory schema, then something else emerges: the relationality of God. In the Jewish Bible/OT, the identities of God and Israel are a matter of who they are to each other. At the same time, neither is reducible to this relation. God is the holy one. Israel is a community of people who can and do both accept and reject a relationship with God on God's terms. Power is not, of course, absent from the biblical picture. Yet power is also curiously refracted through a pattern of mutuality or reciprocity in a way that sidelines or relativizes any exclusive claim to it.

3 Divinity in the World

The period I'm calling Heidegger's "thirties" (following Polt) was characterized by crisis, self-revision, and a kind of self-imposed intellectual isolation. During this time Heidegger tried to come out against what he viewed as mistaken philosophical interpretations of National Socialism, albeit in the name of the "inner truth and greatness" of the latter. At the same time, he labored in private on thousands pages of notes, sketches, and essayistic pieces, none of which was published during their author's lifetime. In Section 2, I pursued one possible line of inquiry into Heidegger's work from these years. Another discernible strand of thinking running through Heidegger's writings at this time is a strident, sometimes embittered, attack on Christianity as metaphysics and as "cultural claim" [*Kulturanspruch*]. In the *Black Notebooks* from these dark years, Heidegger's denunciations begin with the Concordat of 1933, for which he lambastes both Church and Nazi leadership, and extend to the end of the war, the destructiveness of which in his view demonstrated the "feebleness" of the "Christian God [*Christengott*]." Heidegger retains this generally dim view of Christianity throughout the next decade. He repeatedly decries the "atheism" of philosophy and theology (GA 98, 224; 230; 246). A passage written later in the 1950s nicely captures the heart of Heidegger's critique: "[i]f God is represented as the *highest* [*oberste*] cause, then it seems that God is being recognized in his loftiness [*Hoheit*]; but [in fact] he is being debased to godlessness. Nothing of God's divinity belongs to the 'first cause.' Representing God as the highest of all causes is pledging allegiance to pure atheism" (GA 100, 37; cf. GA 100, 130).

As ever with Heidegger, this apparent repudiation of Christianity is not simply negative, simply a matter of denying that God exists. Amidst one of the many passages decrying Christianity, Heidegger approvingly notes how his thought has been characterized as "atheism," for indeed "a thoughtful sparing [*Schonung*] of divinity has nothing at all to do with *their* theism" (GA 98, 23). This suggests that there is something positive about this negative move that Heidegger also wants to articulate in his writings from this early postwar era, albeit something that emerges only from risking godlessness. Heidegger announces that, in the "other inception" of historical being [*Seyn*], just as humanity will no longer be defined metaphysically as "rational animal," likewise God will "cast off his metaphysical-demiurgical essence" (GA 70, 131). In opening up new possibilities for thinking about God, "[o]ther gods do not step into the place of the old, rather, the essence of divinity is something different" (GA 70, 131). But what will God be then? Heidegger being Heidegger, he does not answer this question. But he does explain that, while his philosophy is *not theistic*, it is also not "atheism," since both of these terms secure their meaning within the framework of metaphysics. To attempt to overcome metaphysics, and thus also theism, is not the same as denying God. Perhaps there is something else that can be said about God, about the relationship between human beings and the divine, about how they encounter [*entgegnen*] one another, that can only be discovered once metaphysics has been overcome. That Heidegger explores the possibility that it is so is evidenced by his efforts to reconnect with theologians both Roman Catholic and Protestant during these years. (It could be said that this reengagement marks the passing of Heidegger's "thirties," but that would be speculative.) Even more significant is that Heidegger locates the "divinities" or "godly ones" [*die Göttlichen*] along with "mortals," in the "fourfold" [*Geviert*], the idea that is the keynote of his later thought. Heidegger places the possibility of religion in the age of "positioning" [*Ge-stell*] at the center of his postwar work.

I approach the task of understanding what Heidegger says about matters human and divine in his later works (late 1940s–1950s) in two parts. I begin with a necessarily brief but hopefully illuminating reconstruction of how Heidegger introduces and articulates the "divinities" as he explicates the notion of the "fourfold."[42] I am focusing my investigation specifically on Heidegger's exploration of the possibility of divine–human relation beyond "positioning." I take note of three general features of what Heidegger says in the texts under consideration about how the divine and the human are related, if at all. Briefly, this relation is intra- or inner-worldly (keeping in mind Heidegger's sense of "world" in these texts), orienting, and individuating. The first feature involves

---

[42] For a comprehensive examination of the figure of the "fourfold," see Mitchell 2015.

the common "dependence" of human beings and the divine on historical being, which "worlds" as the "fourfold." The second reflects the way the relation becomes the basis of self-definition within an array of possibilities of meaning. The third feature, individuating, needs to be understood in light of Heidegger's characterization of "identity" as "belonging," such that (1) there is no "higher" or shared universal between what is related, and (2) that which is related is not reduced to the relation. Shared "belonging" does not make that which is related simply *available* or *on order* [*bestellbar*], while it likewise does not leave what is so related completely estranged. That which is related is, Heidegger says, "reflected back" into itself, and so not reducible to its relation to another. The divine and the human share this complex relationship in Heidegger's later thought.

What Heidegger says about all of this is characteristically brief but highly suggestive, which is quite in keeping with Heidegger's insistence that leaving behind *Ge-stell* – "positioning" – requires entering into a situation of indeterminacy. Heidegger usually does not say anything more specific about the divinities than is needed to sketch out the "mirror-play" of the "fourfold." But he sometimes speaks in more specific terms. I recall here the important remarks made in an appendix to the published version (1954) of an earlier (1949) address, "The Thing." Heidegger relates an answer to a friendly query, giving several hints as to what he has in mind when he speaks in the essay of the "divinities" who "beckon" or "hint." One striking inclusion in the list is the "preaching of Jesus" (GA 7, 185). Heidegger being Heidegger, it is a fair bet that the genitive in this phrase is both subjective (Jesus's preaching, e.g., in parables or in the Sermon on the Mount) and objective (the teaching or message *about* Jesus). Taking up this pointer from Heidegger, the last part of this section explores who Jesus is, what he says, and what is said about him in the gospel of Mark, thus exhibiting one way of trying to understand what Heidegger means by the "divinities."

3.1 Excursus on Heidegger and "Atheism"

As already mentioned, Heidegger's *Black Notebooks* from the late 1940s and 1950s are replete with passages in which he denounces the "atheism" of theologians. Perhaps recalling Nietzsche's announcement of the death of God in *Gay Science*, Heidegger avers at one point that "the maddest [*tollste*] atheism that has ever [*jemals*] come into the world consists in the demand for and attempt at proofs of God" (GA 98, 246). While the tone is somewhat softer in his published writings, there is still clearly a critical edge to Heidegger's discussions of conventional metaphysical theology, which, by 1949, Heidegger has folded into the notion of "positioning" [*Ge-stell*]. In an oft-cited passage from *Identity and Difference* (1957), Heidegger writes: "[*Causa sui*] is the proper name for God in philosophy. A human being can neither petition nor sacrifice to this God. Before the *causa sui*, a human being can neither fall awestruck to his knees, nor play music and dance (GA 11, 90)".

Here, rather than accuse metaphysical theologians of outright "atheism," Heidegger *merely* says that what they're talking about is not God, but something else that, unlike God, inspires no devotion. Elsewhere, Heidegger maintains a different criticism of classical, metaphysical theology, i.e., that it calculates. From around the time in which he authored the *Contributions to Philosophy* and thereafter, Heidegger uses the label "calculating" [*rechnen*] to encompass an expansive range of ways of reasoning (GA 65, 35; 40–41; 72; 91; et passim). "To calculate" means, variously, to deduce, to reason instrumentally, to explain (in a scientific sense), and to deliberate.[43] The "atheism" of metaphysical theology, at least in part, consists in the fact that it involves or requires "calculating" about God. Heidegger is suggesting there is something amiss with the project of reasoning about God. Without exploring these various remarks in detail, I will simply observe that it is probably best not to read these accusations of atheism literally, in the sense of "denying the existence of God." Instead, Heidegger is trying to rhetorically motivate the "leap" (see Section 2) into or toward a new possibility for thinking about God. It is not a question of there being a better description of God, nor of the strength of the argument(s) in favor of this new approach. These are ways of thinking about what philosophy offers that are exogenous to Martin Heidegger's project. He wants us to see something like the following: Thinking about God in terms of metaphysics is a dry well, it is played out, exhausted, now just a question of "ordering up" [*bestellen*] useful ideas for whatever purpose. So, if we want to think about God, which Heidegger clearly intends for us to do, we'll have to do it in a new way.

3.2 Worldifying the Divine

The most striking evidence for Heidegger's ongoing interest in thinking about religion during the postwar years comes from writings authored between 1949 and 1951, some of which were later published in 1954 in the volume *Addresses and Essays* (GA 7). It is in these texts that Heidegger first publicly sets forth his account of the "fourfold," the signal idea from this period of his thought.

---

[43] See GA 65, 35; 40–41; 72; 91; et passim. For a passage in the *Contributions* that links calculating with machination and representational thinking, see GA 65, 108–110. This connection is made once again in notebooks from the late 1940's (GA 98, 65).

"Fourfold" is, to be brief, a name for a totality of relations between dimensions of meaning that constitute the meaning that things have. Importantly for the present investigations, these dimensions include one referred to as the "divinities" [*die Göttlichen*]. A helpful reference point from Heidegger's thought that helps to explicate this later notion of the "fourfold" is the concept of "world." While Heidegger's use of "world" evolved over time, the overarching notion at work is that of such a totality or network of relations of significance.[44] These relations are not reducible to empirical properties of things. Rather, things (and people) "stand out" by way of pointing to different possibilities of meaning which they can come to have for various ways of doing things (including thinking about them). Similarly, the "divinities" in the "fourfold" point beyond themselves to something that is not immediately given but which can come to be reflected in the performance of a new mode of human existence, "dwelling." The ways in which things can indicate the divine are only apparent in the midst of this activity. As I discussed in Section 1, in the early 1920s Heidegger began to explore a conception of life as unfolding in the midst of various "worlds" – the environment [*Umwelt*], with-world [*Mitwelt*], self-world [*Selbst-welt*]. Rather than being thought in terms of spatial dimensions, these "worlds" are dimensions of meaning that are unified in the performance [*Vollzug*] of a life. Heidegger makes it clear that the "fourfold" is a way of saying something about "world" in this distinct sense of the term: world "worlds" as the "fourfold" (GA 79, 19; 181).

The "fourfold," then, consists in four dimensions of meaning that make possible the meaningful presence of things in our lives. These four dimensions are earth, sky, mortals, and divinities [*die Göttlichen*]. Keeping in mind Heidegger's *performative* approach to philosophy, it is probably best not to think of "fourfold" as literally descriptive of something; the relations he is talking about are not "properties" of "things." Likewise, Heidegger makes clear that "fourfold" is also not properly thought of as *cause* or *condition*. Instead, what Heidegger is doing is indicating the shape of a performance, the performance of a way of living that he styles "dwelling" during this period. The "fourfold" is not somehow separate from "dwelling," but rather it is embedded, as it were, within it. The "fourfold" is the shape that "dwelling" has. It is clear also that Heidegger, in his talk of the "divinities" in the "fourfold," is not making assertions about the

---

[44] Several stages or periods in Heidegger's ongoing reflections about "world" can be identified: (1) the three "worlds" (self-, with-, and surrounding) of factical life (in the early 1920s); (2) "world" as network of references (*Being and Time*, esp. § 18); (3) "world" as the structure of Dasein's "transcendence" (late 1920s); (4) "world" in the account of the artwork (second half of the 1930s); and (5) "world" as the "fourfold" (late 1940s and 1950s). Heidegger is not saying the same thing over again in each of these instances; the concept "world" undergoes revision, expansion, and reconfiguration across the length of Heidegger's career.

existence of some being or beings, but is, once again, pointing to a dimension of meaning in relation to which the performance of a life unfolds.

The "fourfold" notably includes "divinities." Heidegger accordingly envisions a way of living that incorporates a *divine* dimension, in contrast to life under the dominant framework of "positioning [*Ge-stell*]." I am interested here in articulating the positive possibilities for thinking about religion opened up by Heidegger. It must be acknowledged that separating the subject matter out in this manner from the larger context of the "fourfold" is foreign to how Heidegger himself carries out his reflections. It is also true that the precise meaning of the "divinities" is a matter of disagreement among scholars. Roughly, the scholarship divides between those who want to emphasize a largely or wholly *secularized* understanding of this term, and those who want to maintain its religious connotations. Here I will take it for granted that, when Heidegger talks of the *divinities*, he is talking about the religious dimension of a possible way of living.

It is significant in this respect that Heidegger distinguishes between "secularization [*Säkularisierung*]" and "worldifying [*Verweltlichung*]" in unpublished notebooks from the late 1940s.

> Worldifying: that being [*das Sein*] enters [*einkehrt*] the worlding of the world, which requires first of all that world be adapted [*sich ereignen*], cleared in its essence, and everything present comes into its own within it [*in dieses enteignen*]. (GA 98, 102)

> Secularization: that within metaphysics and Christendom [*Christentum*] sheer human action and production have gained the upper hand, and make use in this manner of the Christian revelation, and picture it as an ethical doctrine [*Sittenlehre*]. (GA 98, 102)[45]

Talk of "worldifying," I take it, points to a way of thinking non-metaphysically about how things become present, intelligible, and available for us through the unfolding of a world, of a totality of relations of significance. Heidegger is indicating that it is this "worldifying," or "making worldly," that interests him, *rather than* secularization. To "worldify" the divine is not to reduce it to something else, or even to make divinity a discernible "property" of a "thing." "Divinities" are not in the "world" in the sense of being reducible to something non-divine (physical or psychological); rather, they belong, *as divine*, to the network of relations of meaning that all worldly (in the standard, non-Heideggerian sense) things presuppose. "Divinity" is the way, within human

---
[45] My translation of *enteignen* as "come into its own" follows suggestions found in Hirsch 1978. Hirsh points out how the prefix *ent-* has multiple senses, and that the more literal "expropriate" does not fit the contexts in which it is used.

activity and against a whole background of relations of meaning, that a thing can point beyond itself to something more complete or "whole [*heil*]"

Perhaps a more direct way of getting to this point is to observe how Heidegger introduces the "divinities" in the address (and later essay) "The Thing." The ceramic jug, the eponymous "thing" of the title, is essentially what it is in "pouring." Heidegger writes:

> The gift of the pour is the drink for mortals. It quenches their thirst. It enlivens their leisure time. It brings joy to their socializing. But the gift of the jug will also, from time to time, be dedicated to consecrated use [*zur Weihe*]. If the pour is for consecrated use, then it does not quench a thirst. It satisfies the observance of the festival on high..... The pour is the drink spilled out by mortals for the divinities. (GA 79, 11–12)[46]

In the performance of different activities (having a party, invoking the god), the meaning of an ordinary thing gets configured in a certain way. This meaning can either be oriented mainly to the divine or to the human, but this is because the thing can be located within a network of possibilities that become actual by way doing something. The thing, in this case the ceramic jug, "gathers" mortals and divinities, who "each [*je*] tarry in a different way," and yet are "entrusted" [*zugetraut*] to one another. The same holds good for all four dimensions of the "fourfold." "Each of the four in its way reflects back [*spiegelt . . . wieder*] the essence of the rest. Each is thus in its way reflected back [*spiegelt sich . . . zurück*] into what is its own within the singleness of the four. This mirroring is no presentation of an image" (GA 79, 19). Heidegger's talk of "reflecting back into oneself" and being "entrusted" to another is meant to suggest, I think, that the different realms of meaning do not reduce to their relation to one another. The divine and the human remain what they are while being related through the performance of some specific activity, such as pouring liquid out onto the ground from a vessel. The "world" in the sense of the "mirror-play" of the "fourfold" is not a cause or ground, nor are the four related to each other as cause or ground of each other. Divinities belong *in the world*, which is itself not their cause or ground; they are likewise not the cause or ground of the world (GA 79, 19). Heidegger's talk of *Verweltlichung* does not involve deleting religion or the sacred from life, or replacing these with something else. On the contrary, it means that divinities and mortals *share* the world, though in the sense of the "fourfold." For "world" is "the still

---

[46] In the original: "In der Guß zur Weihe, dann stillt er nicht einen Durst. Er stillt die Feier des Festes ins Hohe" (G79, 12). Much of what Heidegger says in these postwar essays about the divine recalls "Wie wenn am Feiertage," an address published in 1941 (G4). Note the recurrence of (religious) observance [*die Feier*], for example.

concealed mirror-play of the fourfold of heaven and earth, mortals and divinities" (GA 79, 47).

As I have urged previously, it is very helpful to think of Heidegger in these texts as talking nondescriptively, as indicating or pointing to a possible way of living (e.g., GA 98, 62–63). The sense of what he is saying can be brought out contrastively by considering what Heidegger has to say about the way things go during late modernity, which is summed up by the term *das Ge-stell*, "positioning." In the address of that title from 1949, Heidegger explains how "positioning" makes possible "ordering up" or "putting in an order" [*bestellen*] for anything that could be said to "be." To be just is to be put in place [*gestellt*], inventoried, made available for order. This includes both "nature and history, the human and the divine" (GA 79, 31). In fact, it is *Ge-stell*, "positioning," that is at work in the errors that Heidegger elsewhere denounces as "atheism." What Heidegger says in the essay points to a further way of understanding the charge of atheism. Metaphysical theology fundamentally mistakes God because it depends upon God's being "positioned" [*gestellt*] in an inventory of concepts. Hence, Heidegger writes that "if today an ill-advised theology orders up for itself the results of modern atomic physics in order to secure, with their help, its proofs for God, then God is thereby placed in the domain of the orderable [*Bestellbaren*]" (GA 79, 31).

Ge-stell functions to "ensnare" or "entrap [*Nachstellen*]" "world," meaning that, like metaphysics in Heidegger's writings from the "thirties," it sets up a rigid schema that conceals other background possibilities (GA 79, 53). *Ge-stell, bestellen, bestellbar, nachstellen* are all terms that obviously share the verbal root *stellen*. In 1920–1921, it will be recalled, Heidegger had critically examined the role of yet another cognate, *Einstellung*, in blocking access to the performative meaning of the Situation. In the address entitled "The Danger," Heidegger explains that *stellen* means what in Greek is called *thesis*. In the Greek way of thinking, according to Heidegger, *physis* is the condition for *thesis*, in the sense that things must be first "displayed" or "brought forth" in order for anything to be erected [*hingestellt*] with them by means of humans "positioning" [*stellen*] them (GA 79, 64). The historical shape of this relation is variable, but Heidegger maintains that the way we late moderns engage things requires that they first of all be capable of being "requisitioned" [*bestellt*]. What Heidegger is hinting at when he talks of the "divinities" in the "fourfold" is an altogether different state of affairs, in which relationships between the divine and the human do not first of all require "positioning" [*Ge-stell*]. In this situation, things cannot be reduced to their position in the inventory, but point beyond themselves to possibilities that cannot be calculated in advance but must be performed in order to be understood. Much in the way he had urged in 1920–1921 the suspension of an objectifying attitude [*Einstellung*] in order to reperform the original performance of Christian life, so here in the early 1950s Heidegger suggests the possibility of giving up on "positioning" as a condition for relating to the divine. The situation of the divine in the era of "positioning" is such that radical change is all that can secure it a meaningful place in life:

> The divinity of God has long since been misrecognized [*verkannt*]. The path to it has been fundamentally covered over and concealed by "lived experience," through which everyone drank deeply of the isolated or, even more so, the collective I-hood, or the I-Thou relation. The divinity of the god has become a content of lived experience, and so an inventory item [*Bestand*] for ordering up lived experiences [*Erlebnisbestellung*]. Where there are only machines running, the hegemony of *Ge-stell* is obvious, but when, in a way hidden from public view, the divinity becomes an inventory item for ordering, the uncanniness of *Ge-stell* has its most dangerous shape, when let loose inconspicuously. An example: someone now tries to ascertain through a survey in a large daily newspaper whether a religious renewal will happen soon. On this basis, one persuades oneself to take part in furthering the "religious" in this way. (GA 98, 406)

In a key essay of 1951, "Building, Dwelling, Thinking," Heidegger repeats his earlier characterization of the "divinities" as "the beckoning [*winkenden*] messengers of the divinity [*Gottheit*]" (GA 7, 152). "The divinity," or "the God," has his own domain that does not reduce to these "messengers," who only point beyond themselves. The God both "appears into his presence and withdraws into his concealment" (GA 7, 152).[47] God is both hidden and revealed, unavailable, and yet not absent. The "divinities" are like gestures, signs, or pointers, and so are referred to something beyond them that they make present without simply making available. To greet or say farewell with a wave both makes one present to another and maintains distance; likewise with pointing to something else. For their part, mortals are brought into relation with the divine by the "beckoning" of the "divinities," and are drawn out of themselves in this way.[48] The "divinities" are not simply available to mortals, for they relate to the latter by way of the distance-preserving gesture. While they further point beyond themselves to an even further possibility, they also remain separate from it, and do not make it wholly present. Heidegger is conceiving of the

---
[47] Mitchell 2015 helpfully explicates the meaning of this "beckoning."
[48] This is also a point anticipated by Heidegger in "Wie wenn am Feiertage," where he says about "the holy" that it "confronts all experience with something to which it is unaccustomed, and so deprives it of its ground. Deranging [*ent-setzend*] in this way, the holy is the awesome [*Entsetzliche*] itself" (G4, 63).

significance of things as being located "beyond" or "outside" of them, in relation to possibilities that are only understood in performing some activity. The meaning of something is not exhausted by any one possibility of engagement with it. In like manner, the divinities do not collapse into their relation to the mortals, nor vice versa. The "divine" possibilities of things themselves point to something further beyond themselves that cannot be reduced to its relation to them or to its relation, via them, to mortals. The relation between divinities and mortals in this way *individuates* what is related.

Mortals are likewise distinguished by the relation to the divine, for it is how they themselves receive the hints of the "divinities" that precisely constitutes their difference from the "divinities." How do mortals "dwell" in relation to the "divinities"?

> Mortals dwell in that they await divinities as divinities. In hope they hold up to the divinities what is unhoped for. They wait for the hints of their arrival and do not overlook the signs of their absence. They do not make gods for themselves and do not worship idols. In the very depth of misfortune they wait for the weal that has been withdrawn [*Im Unheil noch warten sie des entzogenes Heils*]. (GA 7, 152)

Heidegger characterizes the reception of the "divinities" in terms of *waiting* and *hope* – indeed, hope beyond hope, desperate hope, hope for what is unhoped for. Without claiming any direct connection, one can hardly help being reminded of Heidegger's exposition of Christian hope in the apocalyptic Situation from 1920–1921. What is important to note is that expectancy, waiting, and, more especially, hope make something or someone present even while, and precisely because, it or they are absent; "hope that is seen is not hope" (Rom. 8:24). Furthermore, to have hope or expectancy is to move beyond oneself, to have one's self in what has not yet arrived. Recalling how Paul lauds the Thessalonians for having turned away from "idols" (1 Thess. 1:9), here Heidegger suggests that this hopeful attitude is joined to a kind of loyalty to what is yet hidden or has yet to arrive. Hopefulness and loyalty are how mortals "dwell," that is, how they take up a position in relational totality of the "fourfold," and thus how it is that they *orient* their lives toward the divine.

The stance or orientation toward the divine that Heidegger is calling "dwelling" is not conceptual, theoretical, or a question of "worldview." Rather, how mortals "dwell" conditions how things show up as significant. Heidegger illustrates this point in the essay "Building Dwelling Thinking":

> Now in the high arch, now in a low, the bridge vaults over glen and stream – whether mortals keep in mind this vaulting of the bridge's course or forget that they, always themselves on their way to the last bridge, are actually

striving to surmount all that is common and unsound in them in order to bring themselves before the haleness of the divinities. The bridge *gathers*, as a passage that crosses, before the divinities – whether we explicitly think of, and visibly *give thanks for*, their presence, as in the figure of the saint of the bridge, or whether that divine presence is obstructed or even pushed wholly aside. (GA 7, 155)

Here, Heidegger reminds us how the relation between divinities and mortals distinguishes them from each other and individuates them. Mortals are not somehow constrained to take note of the divine and their unique relationship to it; that there is anything divine is by no means obvious, but requires the performance of a certain way of life in order to notice. Mortals and divinities can and do go their own ways, and yet their relation is still in play. It is also worth pointing out how the bridge, for Heidegger, reflects the distinctive identity of the mortals, i.e., their mortality. Once again, the mortals and divinities are not reducible to or identical with one another, but each retains a sphere of possibility inaccessible to the other. Heidegger suggests that, for the divine, what is its own is a kind "wholeness" beyond what is mortally possible. Calling to mind any of the many stone bridges that cross southern Germany's rivers and streams, often appointed with a statue of St. Jan Nepomuk, Heidegger again points to the stance of mortals to divinities, this time bringing out *thankfulness* and *recollection*. These, too, are ways of making someone or something present while maintaining its absence or distance. In order to comport oneself this way toward something or someone else, a relation must already be in play in the background, one has to be already "there," as it were, with the other one. This is the point Heidegger is making in his discussion of *physis* and *thesis* described earlier. World has to "world" before any possible comportment to things can be realized. In this way, "divinities" and mortals could be said to depend upon world worlding, though, Heidegger insists, not in a causal way.

That there is, to echo *Being and Time*, "always already" some relation to the divinities, whether recognized in hope, loyalty, thankfulness, or not, that co-constitutes what it is to be "mortal," is an idea Heidegger also draws on from his reading of Hölderlin. In the address "... dichterisch wohnet der Mensch," delivered on several occasions in the early 1950s and likewise published in *Addresses and Essays*, Heidegger takes fragments of work by Hölderlin as the launching point for his most detailed discussion of the divine human relationship during this period of his thought. Whether it is acknowledged or not, some relation to the divine is constitutive of what it is to be human (GA 7, 199). Hence, Hölderlin's line "Der Mensch misset sich ... mit der Gottheit."[49]

---

[49] I choose to leave Hölderlin's poetry untranslated here.

Heidegger's immediate gloss on this line is as follows: "[The divinity] is 'the measure [*Maaß*],' with which the human being sizes up [*ausmißt*] his dwelling, his sojourn on the earth beneath heaven. Only insofar as the human being thus surveys [*ver-mißt*] his dwelling is he able to fittingly *be* his essence (GA 7, 199)".

Heidegger being Heidegger, it is safe to think that he is employing variations on the root *messen*, "to measure," to articulate something about this background relation between the human and divine. The overall sense Heidegger is conveying would seem to involve locating oneself and marking off spaces for other things in relation to oneself. Heidegger thinks the kind of measuring he is describing is disconnected from mathematically precise measurement in geometry and land surveying (GA 7, 199). The "surveying" is rather what allows "dwelling" to enter into its unfolding "plan" or "blueprint" or "outline [*Grundriß*]" – less a rigid schema than a safe place [*Gewähr*] in which mortal dwelling "endures" [*währt*] (GA 7, 199). In this sense, the measuring is creative or generative, marking off spaces of possibility. It is also something mortals have to do or to perform – they must "take the measure" of something in order to set up these spaces of possibility.

Continuing gloss on Hölderlin's fragment, Heidegger explores how divinity [*Gottheit*] could be the "measure" that humans take in plotting their lives. The issue is that God is "hidden," not accidentally, but precisely insofar as God *is* God. God is unfamiliar, strange, nameless, foreign – all connotations of Hölderlin's word, *unbekannt*. At first pass, it is difficult to see how what is *unbekannt* could really function as a "measure" in the way that Hölderlin seems to be saying it must. After all, in order to function as required, something must appear, communicate itself, and in so doing becoming *bekannt*, familiar. Heidegger acknowledges that the idea of something being familiar (apparent) and unfamiliar (hidden) at the same time would conflict with common sense, "which likes to assert itself as the correct measure for all thinking and reflecting" (GA 7, 201). But he and Hölderlin are starting from a different place, from the fact that being *unbekannt* requires that whatever is *unbekannt* in some way shows itself as *unbekannt*. Speaking of God, the point is therefore that "he appears as the one who remains unfamiliar" (GA 7, 201).

It's fair to say that Heidegger's principal interest in this fascinating late essay is to understand what Hölderlin is saying about poetic creation, about *Dichtung*. And so he reflects on how it is that the poet takes up and "imagines [*einbildet*]" or "depicts" these appearances of God as unfamiliar or strange (GA 7, 191–196, 204). My focus, in contrast, is on the relationship between the human and the divine that Heidegger unearths in these fragmentary verses by Hölderlin. What Heidegger outlines is a style of thinking that is receptive to hints, gestures, suggestions of the divine, while avoiding any attempt at a "grasp" [*Zugriff*]. The unknown [*unbekannt*] is able to be made known [*bekannt*] by something that lets what is "self-concealing appear in self-unveiling" (GA 7, 205). In Hölderlin's poem, such an "unveiling that allows what conceals itself to be seen" is accomplished by "heaven" or the "clouds of heaven" (GA 7, 201). But this is hardly intended to be the exclusive locus of divine revelation, which expands here to include all that is "familiar," "trusted," and "intimate" [*Vertraute*]:

> Everything in heaven, under heaven, and on the earth that glows and blooms, resounds and is fragrant, rises up and approaches, but also falls and passes by, that cries out and remains silent, grows lighter and darkens. Into what is intimately familiar in this manner to the human, and yet is strange to God, what is unknown [*unbekannt*] sends itself in order to remain sheltered in [what is intimately familiar] as the unknown. (GA 7, 205)

What can be learned from "... dichterisch wohnet der Mensch ..." and other texts composed between 1949 and 1951 about how Heidegger thinks about the possibilities of religion in his late work? The divine and the human share the "world," they co-belong to it, in two senses. First, they comprise part of the constitutive relationships of sense that allow things to be significant in life. In their noncausal, nonreductive "mirroring" relation, divinities and humans (along with earth and sky) "gather" or constitute the various ways in which ordinary things, like ceramic jugs and bridges, are meaningful to us (or how these things "thing"). Second, divinities and humans share a dependence on the worlding of world, which makes possible their mutual relatedness. At the same time, the relation to the divinities orients mortals, or gives them a "measure" [*Maaß*] in light of which they construct their lives. Heidegger characterizes this basic orientation in terms of *hope, loyalty, thankfulness, recollection*, and other stances that involve ways of making present something that remains not fully accessible. These are ways of bringing oneself into relation to something or someone else while respecting the insurmountable distance. Heidegger likewise reflects, in light of some late versus by Hölderlin, on how the divinities relate to mortals without being reduced to this relation. The relationship both connects or unites and individuates what is related. God is *revealed* as what is as such unknown, hidden, or obscure. The everyday ken of humanity, the familiar "sights" of life, are the context or backdrop against which what is *essentially* strange or unfamiliar can appear as such.

3.3 The Hidden Christ

I previously pointed out a clue Heidegger gives in the published version of "Das Ding" (1954) about examples of what he means by "the divinities" in his late work. Alongside the gods of Greece and "prophetic Judaism," Heidegger cited the "preaching of Jesus." A longer note, composed sometime in 1949 or 1950, as Heidegger was working through a series of addresses and essays outlining his later thinking, seems to probe in the same direction as the clue presented in the published volume. Also discussed previously in this section is how, elsewhere in the same set of notes, Heidegger draws a distinction between his own thinking and any effort at "secularization." Here, he seems to want to differentiate *Christentum* – perhaps, "Christendom" – from *die Christliche* – what is Christian. Heidegger had relied on a notion of "what is Christian" before, for example, in the essay "Phenomenology and Theology" from the late 1920s (GA 9, 45). Concerning what is Christian, Heidegger now (1949–1950) notes the following:

> *The Christian* – if we understand by that the life and preaching of Jesus, the relation to the world experienced and set forth [*ausgetragene*] by Jesus, then this [sense of] "Christian" is prior to all reinterpretation [*Umdeutung*] of Jesus as Christ. The Christian is then in truth the pre-Christian and perhaps in a certain way is thus outside the metaphysical – outside perhaps, but never [the same as] the winding back of the history of being. This means that the contemporary person, if he is still of a mind [*gesonnen*] to be "Christian," must return to the pre-Christian life of Jesus. Perhaps thinking could indirectly be a helpful occasion for this return to the pre-Christian, which is different from primal Christianity [*Ur-Christentum*] – a thinking that in its manner defers to the winding back of the essence of metaphysics and points to a free place [*ins Freye*] without presuming to insert itself into the pre-Christian. Perhaps simply thinking could be more helpful to this return to the pre-Christian than all theology and metaphysics of transcendence. (GA 98, 103)

One thing that can be gathered from this passage and the others discussed previously is that Heidegger is suggesting or hinting at the possibility of thinking about Jesus non-metaphysically and nondogmatically. He had made related suggestions and hints in "Phenomenology and Theology," and elsewhere. What follows here is one way to follow up on the hints Heidegger gives here in notebooks from the late 1940s. For Heidegger, thinking about Jesus non-metaphysically means thinking about him as exemplifying the "divine." The "divine," it will be recalled, is characterized as a "beckoning messenger," and I explored the interplay of presence and absence in beckoning and in communicating a message. Furthermore, I have noted how Heidegger follows Hölderlin in pointing to the "unfamiliar [*unbekannt*]" standing out against yet encompassed by the everyday, by the "familiar" [*bekannt*]. The divine appears *as* hidden or obscure, and in that way is not reducible to its appearance. Heidegger also investigates the thought that responding to these gestures involves ways of "imagining" [*einbildet*] them or trying to depict them that does not provide simple "access" [*Zugriff*]. These are all thoughts that are intended by Heidegger to be further hints or gestures themselves. There is no system, nor doctrine, that is being set forth. Nothing particularly requires that these gestures be followed, and with Heidegger's elusive prose as a guide it will be easy to make a mistake. That is all just to say that, in what follows, I am not ascribing to Heidegger some view about, in this case, the Gospel of Mark, or about Christology. Instead, I am following up on the possibility of thinking of the divine non-metaphysically and nondoctrinally.

It was once a commonplace of critical scholarship that the second Gospel, Mark, used a device called "the Messianic Secret" to try to convey something about who Jesus was.[50] Something like this view was widely held, for example, by the then up-to-date critical scholars that Heidegger studied in the 1910s. It is no longer the case that the consensus of critical scholarship supports the hypothesis of the "Messianic Secret."[51] Yet none deny that one of the characteristic features of Mark's Gospel is the way in which Jesus's identity is obscure to many of those whom he encounters in the story, while he sternly charges others to keep his identity a secret. Mark depicts Jesus as very often hidden or withdrawn from view, while at the same time being very much publicly present, beset by throngs of people and peppered with questions meant to test his piety. When Jesus tries, eventually, to say who he is more directly, he seemingly cannot be understood. No one can quite get a handle on the idea of a giver who gives himself away, and who is rejected, who identifies with the invisible, weak, and small. The motif of the hidden yet destined to be revealed messianic figure, the Son of Man, is a recognizable aspect of apocalyptic writing, and it is present in Mark as well. The "Similitudes of Enoch" (1 Enoch 48:3–7, 62:7), a late addition to the most important pseudepigraphical source for understanding Jewish apocalypticism, portray such a figure. The estimated late date (first century CE) of this work makes it part of the general milieu of the author of the Gospel of Mark. At the same time, the evangelist employs these traditions to a distinctive end and in a distinctive manner.

In Mark, Jesus is often shown as hidden and withdrawn, often to the wilderness or mountains. For instance, after his baptism by John the Baptist, Jesus

---

[50] This idea was originated by the great Wilhelm Wrede, most fully in *Das Messiasgeheimnis in der Evanglium* (1901). For an English edition, see Wrede 1971. The original thought is that, since actual, historical Jesus would not (or did not, or could not?) have designated himself the Messiah or Christ, the author of Mark, in order to make that very claim about Jesus, had to make up a subplot about how Jesus conceals the truth about who he is, thus explaining why no one had ever heard about it before. It is perhaps historical "insights" such as this that Heidegger alludes to in his well-known letter to Engelbert Krebs as having led him to renounce the "system of Catholicism." In a dramatic twist, it is rumored that Wrede himself renounced this idea late in life.

[51] A very informative collection dealing with the history of this idea and related matters is Tucket 1983.

withdraws to what is referred to as a "deserted place" to pray. His anxious followers frantically track him down (Mark 1: 36–37). He sometimes turns away those who would be his followers (5:19–20). At the same time, Jesus is publicly present, encountering people in ways that cannot be secret, and interacting with them in the midst of the everyday. Twice in Mark's Gospel, Jesus performs the very public act of feeding a huge crowd of people (6:21–44; 8:1–10). It is not just the number of people involved that should be noted here; Jesus relates to people by providing their basic, *ordinary*, physical needs, and by healing people of conditions that debarred them from leading *ordinary* lives. Jesus is also publicly present in the sense that he has a social identity and kinship ties; for some, he's a hometown boy (6:3). Jesus makes himself known to his followers in the midst of their everyday labors, on the docks, or in the toll booth (2:14). Yet, despite all of these ways of being present, Jesus remains hidden. Sometimes, Mark recounts how it is Jesus himself who insists on a degree of anonymity, even while doing eye-catching things. For example, among his neighbors and kin in Capernaum, Jesus heals a demoniac. The departing spirit names Jesus "the Holy One of God," only to be commanded to keep silent. Meanwhile, people who witness all of this seem perplexed and doubtful about what to say regarding who Jesus is (1:27). This pattern continues in the Gospel, where Mark describes how, as he traveled, Jesus "would not permit the demons to speak, because they knew him" (1:34). "Whenever the unclean spirits saw him, they fell down before him and shouted, 'You are the Son of God!' But he sternly ordered them not to make him known" (3:11–12). At other times, unprompted by demonic recognition, Jesus keeps out of the public eye, not wanting anyone to know when he enters the city of Tyre (7:24), or even as he travels through his homeland of Galilee (9:30). It is important not to forget to credit the author of Mark with a keen sense of the ironic; while no one else seems to know who Jesus is, his demonic enemies identify him. Furthermore, the intended readers of the Gospel would be those who precisely proclaim the truth of what the departing demons shout. The irony reaches a peak at the end of the story, first of all when Jesus is mockingly crowned by the soldiers, who of course are unknowingly acknowledging his true identity (15:16–20). The *titulus* that declares Jesus's supposed crime is likewise intended as a mocking insult, yet it winds up announcing the truth (15:25). So, too, the hostile crowd that comes to jeer and insult the crucified man sarcastically call out to him as "Messiah, the King of Israel" (15:32). The final irony comes as the Roman soldier confesses Jesus's true identity when he observes his death (15:39).[52]

---

[52] Yet a further level of irony emerges into view when the Hellenistic and Roman concern with "dying well" is taken into account. The manner of a person's death and their conduct during the process of meeting with their death either express virtue or reveal a person's lackluster character.

The preachings of Jesus, both the content of his message and the manner of delivery, similarly work to make present something that remains ultimately hidden or not fully discernible. Mark portrays Jesus as saying some things very directly that no one seems to understand. This happens for the first time in the following passage:

> Then he began to teach them that the Son of Man must undergo great suffering and be rejected by the elders, the chief priests, and the scribes, and be killed, and after three days rise again. *He said all this quite openly.* And Peter took him aside and began to rebuke him. But turning and looking at his disciples, he rebuked Peter and said, "Get behind me, Satan! For you are setting your mind not on divine things but on human beings." (8:31–33; emphasis mine)

Jesus is required to reiterate this seemingly unthinkable thought (9:12, 9:30, 10:34, 10:45). The difficulty that Peter and others are having turns out to be the result of how "divine things" of which Jesus speaks are the *inversion* of what human beings would expect. He is not describing a possibility that is humanly imaginable. That the Son of Man must suffer is a thought that escapes conventional expectations about what it means to be the Son of Man. This inversion concerns other "divine things" as well. Jesus says shortly after the preceding passage, "those who want to save their life will lose it, and those who lose their life for my sake, and for the sake of the gospel, will save it" (8:35). As the story unfolds, Jesus must also reiterate this reversal or inversion. "Whoever wants to be first must be last of all and servant of all" (9:35). "Many who are first will be last, and the last will be first" (10:31). "Whoever wishes to become great among you must be your servant, and whoever wishes to be first among you must be slave of all. For the Son of Man came not to be served but to serve, and to give his life as a ransom for many" (10:43–45). To paraphrase Paul Ricoeur, it is hard to see how these sayings, taken as they are, could be turned into a manageable life plan under any conventional understanding. There is indeed something *unbekannt*, strange, about the divine things that Jesus is trying to disclose here. The key point to make here is that Jesus's proclamation of the unthinkable is *public*. That is, what he has to say is revealed and yet obscure.

Both what Jesus says and the way in which he often says it function to simultaneously reveal and conceal. In Mark, the parabolic nature of Jesus's style of teaching is often pointed out (3:23, 4:2, 4:33–34, 12:1), sometimes in commentary clearly intended for the reader. The suggestion is often that speaking parabolically is, at least partly, an attempt to deliberately obfuscate something. A great deal of scholarship explores why it might be that Jesus speaks in an indirect, concealing way, and I have no further hypotheses to offer. The

---

The Roman guard proclaims Jesus's exalted status when he sees the manner of his death. Of course, the classical idea of a "good death" most definitely did not include being crucified. See Hengel 1977.

simple fact *that* Jesus uses parables is what is most directly relevant to the present inquiry. When considered on their own, a striking further fact about Jesus's parables is that they locate the hidden in the midst of the everyday. Nothing otherworldly or supernatural, nothing particularly "divine," in fact, is called upon in the parable. Instead, Jesus speaks of someone sowing a field (4:2–9), a farmer (4:26–29), village children (9:35–37, 10:13–16), landlords and tenants (12:1–12), the ripening of cultivated fruit (13:38–31), and a family taking a trip (13:34–35). These ordinary people, places, and occurrences in the parables point to something that is not said out loud, to something so surpassing human ken that it can only be directly expressed by inversions and reversals of the familiar. In the parables, the familiar serves to bring out something surprising, even alienating, about the hidden kingdom of God.

In Mark's Gospel, both Jesus himself – his person, his public, physical presence, his actual life – and Jesus's teachings make God present while at the same time keeping God hidden, obscure, or secret. Who Jesus is remains hidden even from people who know him well (6:49–50, 4:41), while those who do recognize him do so unintentionally or from a point of view beyond the human perspective. What Jesus says, even quite directly and publicly, remains obscure to those who hear him. He likewise speaks in parables and similitudes that contain no hint of the supernatural or supernal, and yet which disclose the divine. In Mark, Jesus is the unknown revealed *as such* in the known. He remains hidden while in public, inaccessible yet present in the mundane. These are aspects of Mark's portrayal of Jesus that would be difficult to capture in terms of familiar conceptual forms. How can something be both public and secret? How can it be ordinary and transcendent? How can it be that Jesus's identity is both hidden and recognized? Heidegger suggests in his late work that these puzzles stem from the habitual adoption of a rigid way of thinking about what it is to be. He likewise urges that this way of thinking is not appropriate for coming to understand the religious dimension of life. Heidegger indicates new possibilities for thinking about the divine and the human, and he even expresses the hope that such possibilities in turn give an impetus to renewed engagement with the divine outside inflexible "positioning" [*Ge-stell*].[53]

Concluding Thoughts

The foregoing discussion is not, and was not intended to be, a comprehensive examination of Heidegger on religion. Heidegger's lifelong explorations of religious ideas and of matters in the neighborhood of religion are extraordinarily

---

[53] Striking passages in Mark have Jesus more or less saying that only someone who undertakes to perform a life *like his own* can understand what he is saying about the kingdom of God. Such an outlook would be familiar to Heidegger, if what I have said so far about his approach to philosophy is on the right track.

rich, and my discussion has focused on just three loci in a vast oeuvre. I have not examined, for example, Heidegger's investigations of non-Western thinking, drawing on traditions such as Buddhism (particularly Zen) and Daoism. Nor have I taken up Heidegger's suggestive discussions of evil, nor of the countervailing notions of "wholeness," "weal," or "soundness," all important themes in his later writings.[54] And, of course, I have comparatively only just brushed up against Heidegger's engagement with Hölderlin's poetic thinking of the divine. I hope, however, that what I have managed to explore in the foregoing sections adds to the impetus to continue to examine these and other aspects of Heidegger's religious thought. I have also urged that this material be approached more in terms of the *spirit* of Heidegger's thought than of the *letter* of it. My suggestion is that taking Heidegger's philosophy nondoctrinally, in an exploratory and *performative* way, is a way to nurture different ways of thinking about religion.

What to say, by way of a general statement, about what has been discussed in the foregoing? The texts that have been examined show Heidegger at work on something that is not a theory of religion, in the sense of a descriptive account of its essence or core function. Nor is it correct to think of Heidegger as mounting a very complicated, not to say convoluted, argument that it is more reasonable than not to believe in God, or to adhere to some religion. In fact, Heidegger seems very often to be at pains to show that ideas about what is reasonable, about what can answer a demand for a reason, in fact cut us off from seeing religion for the *life performance* that it is. All too often, Heidegger maintains, we come to adopt some attitude [*Einstellung*] or other, we try to organize or array phenomena in some supposedly necessary order. The phenomena are further subdivided, as topics of academic study, between different disciplines (e.g., theology, history, psychology, philosophy). Even in many people's daily lives, the sources of meaning are compartmentalized into distinct "experiences." On the basis of observations such as these, Heidegger suggests that we try to suspend or hold in abeyance this tendency to adopt a rigid framework of concepts. Heidegger puts it forward that, if we do that with regard to religion, what we find is not a set of beliefs affirmed by certain individuals, nor a subject matter for sociology, but the performance of the intersection of multiple dimensions of meaning.

If there is anything general that Heidegger himself is trying to say about religion, then it could be that religion necessarily involves risk, uncertainty, and indeterminacy. This is all the more so, Heidegger thinks, in an era witnessing the apotheosis of technical rationality. As a way of being *Da-sein*, religion means

---

[54] Thanks to Eric S. Nelson for suggesting these two examples of parts of Heidegger's corpus that remain unthought in the present study.

being out in the open, exposed, itinerant, and so vulnerable. From his early discussions of Paul on the "distress" and "affliction" of life in the apocalyptic Situation, to his later strictures against making gods for ourselves, Heidegger again and again seeks to deprive religion of comforting certainty. Heidegger is saying that thinking religion, and, more importantly, taking it up into life, both require the same kind of suspension of preconceptions. I have suggested that readers of Heidegger attempt to do the same thing in trying to understand what he is saying. If this attempt is made, Heidegger's thought can be seen less as a closed book than as an experiment (in thinking) that has yet to be run. The goal, for Heidegger, is never to achieve theoretical knowledge of some subject matter, but rather to return to life in its personal, individual (terms Heidegger would eschew) significance which is disclosed in the performance of living.

I have tried to partly run the experiments, as it were, by recruiting the Jewish and Christian scriptures into several of them. It must be admitted that the rationale for this lies primarily in only a single sentence from Heidegger's staggeringly vast oeuvre. That being so, Heidegger himself furnishes a further pointer to how his larger pointer(s) can be followed up. When these traditions, particularly in their Biblical attestations, are explored *da-seinsmäßig*, according to Heidegger's indications of the shape of *Da-sein*, matters such as faith, the nature of God, revelation, and the "final things," show up in a different light. Heidegger's thinking of religion sets into relief the relationality and interplay of presence and absence between human and divine. He envisions a sort of mutuality or reciprocity as well, as opposed to hierarchy and power. It remains what to be seen what else might turn up.

Works by Heidegger

SZ *Sein und Zeit*. Gesamtausgabe, Volume 2. Frankfurt am Main: Klostermann, 1977. English translation: *Being and Time*. Translated by John Macquarrie and Edward Robinson. New York: Harper and Row, 1962.

GA4 *Erläuterungen zu Hölderlins Dichtung*. Gesamtausgabe, Volume 4. Edited by Friedrich-Wilhelm.

von Herrmann. Frankfurt am Main: Klostermann, 1981, 1996. English translation: *Elucidations of Hölderlin's Poetry*. Translated by Keith Hoeller. Amherst, NY: Humanity Books, 2000.

GA6 *Nietzsche*. Gesamtausgabe, Volume 6, 2 Parts. Edited by Birgitte Schillbach. Frankfurt am Main: Klostermann, 1996.

GA7 *Vorträge und Aufsätze*. Edited by Friedrich-Wilhelm von Herrmann. Frankfurt am Main: Klostermann, 2000.

GA9 *Wegmarken*. Gesamtausgabe, Volume 9. Edited by Friedrich-Wilhelm von Herrmann. Frankfurt am Main: Klostermann, 1976. English translation: *Pathmarks*. Edited by William McNeill. Cambridge: Cambridge University Press, 1998.

GA11 *Identität und Differenz*. Gesamtausgabe, Volume 11. Edited by Friedrich-Wilhelm von Herrmann. Frankfurt am Main: Klostermann, 2006.

GA48 *Nietzsche. Der europäische Nihilismus*. Gesamtausgabe, Volume 48. Edited by Petra Jaeger. Frankfurt am Main: Klostermann, 1986.

GA49 *Die Metaphysik der deutschen Idealismus*. Gesamtausgabe, Volume 49. Edited by Günter Seubold. Frankfurt am Main: Klostermann, 2006.

GA52 *Hölderlins Hymne "Andenken."* Gesamtausgabe, Volume 52. Second ed. Edited by Curd Ochwadt. Frankfurt am Main: Klostermann, 1992.

GA58 *Grundprobleme der Phänomenologie*. Gesamtausgabe, Volume 58. Second ed. Edited by Hans-Helmut Gander. Frankfurt am Main: Klostermann, 2010.

GA60 *Phänomenologie des religiösen Lebens*. Gesamtausgabe, Volume 60. Edited by Matthias Jung, Thomas Regehly, Claudius Strube. Frankfurt am Main: Klostermann, 1995.

GA61 *Phänomenologische Untersuchungen zu Aristoteles*. Gesamtausgabe, Volume 61. Edited by Walter Bröcker and Käte Bröcker-Oltmanns. Frankfurt am Main: Klostermann, 1994.

GA63 *Ontologie: Hermeneutik der Faktizität*. Gesamtausgabe, Volume 63. Edited by Käte Bröcker-Oltmanns. Frankfurt am Main: Klostermann, 2018.

GA65 *Beiträge zur Philosophie (vom Ereignis)*. Gesamtausgabe, Volume 65. Edited by Friedrich-Wilhelm von Hermann. Frankfurt am Main: Klostermann, 1989. English translation: *Contributions to Philosophy (Of the Event)*. Translated by Richard Rojcewicz and Daniela Vallega-Neu. Bloomington: Indiana University Press, 2012.

GA66 *Besinnung* (1938–1939). Gesamtausgabe, Volume 66. Edited by Friedrich-Wilhelm von Hermann. Frankfurt am Main: Klostermann, 1997.

GA67 *Metaphysik und Nihilismus*. Gesamtausgabe, Volume 67. Edited by Hans-Joachim Friedrich. Frankfurt am Main: Klostermann, 2018.

GA69 *Die Geschichte des Seyns*. Gesamtausgabe, Volume 69. Edited by Peter Trawny. Frankfurt am Main: Klostermann, 2022.

GA70 *Über den Anfang* (1941). Gesamtausgabe, Volume 70. Edited by Paula-Ludovika Coriando. Frankfurt am Main: Klostermann, 2005.

GA71 *Das Ereignis*. Gesamtausgabe, Volume 71. Edited by Friedrich-Wilhelm von Hermann. Frankfurt am Main: Klostermann, 2009.

GA73 *Zum Ereignis-Denken*. Gesamtausgabe, Volume 73. Two Parts. Edited by Peter Trawny. Frankfurt am Main: Klostermann, 2013.

GA79 *Bremer und Freiburger Vorträge*. Gesamtausgabe, Volume 79. Edited by Petra Jaeger. Frankfurt am Main: Klostermann, 2005.

GA82 *Zu eignen Veröffentlichungen*. Gesamtausgabe, Volume 82. Edited by Friedrich-Wilhelm von Hermann. Frankfurt am Main:Klostermann, 2018.

GA86 *Seminare: Hegel – Schelling*. Gesamtausgabe, Volume 86. Edited by Peter Trawny. Frankfurt am Main: Klostermann, 2011.

GA97 *Anmerkungen I-V (Schwarze Hefte* 1942–1948*)*. Gesamtausgabe, Volume 97. Edited by Peter Trawny. Frankfurt am Main: Klostermann, 2015.

GA98 *Anmerkungen VI-IX (Schwarze Hefte* 1948/49–1951*)*. Gesamtausgabe, Volume 98. Edited by Peter Trawny. Frankfurt am Main: Klostermann, 2018.

GA99 *Vier Hefte I und II (Schwarze Hefte* 1947–1950*)*. Gesamtausgabe, Volume 99. Edited by Peter Trawny. Frankfurt am Main: Klostermann, 2019.

GA100 *Vigiliae und Notturno (Schwarze Hefte* 1952/53–1957*)*. Gesamtausgabe, Volume 100. Edited by Peter Trawny. Frankfurt am Main: Klostermann, 2020.

References

Aner, K. (1964). *Die Theologie der Lessingzeit*. Hildesheim: Georg Olms.
Bambach, C. (2003). *Heidegger's Roots: Nietzsche, National Socialism, and the Greeks*. Ithaca: Cornell University Press.
Brueggemann, W. (1997). *Theology of the Old Testament*. Minneapolis: Fortress Press.
Camilleri, S. (2010). A Historical Note on Heidegger's Relationship to Ernst Troeltsch. In S. McGrath and A. Wiercinski, eds., *A Companion to Heidegger's Phenomenology of Religious Life*. Amsterdam: Brill, 115–134.
Coriando, P., ed. (1998). *Herkunft aber stets bleibt Zukuft: Martin Heidegger und die Gottesfrage*. Frankfurt am Main: Klostermann.
Crowe, B. D. (2006). *Heidegger's Religious Origins: Destruction and Authenticity*. Bloomington: Indiana University Press.
Crowe, B. D. (2007). *Heidegger's Phenomenology of Religion: Realism and Cultural Criticism*. Bloomington: Indiana University Press.
Crowe, B. D. (2019). Hermeneutics and Phenomenology. In M. Forster and K. Gjesdal, eds., *The Cambridge Companion to Hermeneutics*. Cambridge: Cambridge University Press, 211–236.
Crowell, S. (2013). *Normativity and Phenomenology in Husserl and Heidegger*. Cambridge: Cambridge University Press.
Dahlstrom, D. (1994). Heidegger's Method: Philosophical Concepts as Formal Indications. *Review of Metaphysics* 47, 775–795.
Dahlstrom, D. (2001). *Heidegger's Concept of Truth*. Cambridge: Cambridge University Press.
Dahlstrom, D. (2013). *The Heidegger Dictionary*. London: Bloomsbury.
Dahlstrom, D. (2023). *The Heidegger Dictionary*. 2nd ed. London: Bloomsbury.
Eichrodt, W. (1961) and (1967). *Theology of the Old Testament*. 2 Vols. Philadelphia: Westminster Press.
Farias, V. (1991). *Heidegger and Nazism*. Philadelphia: Temple University Press.
Faye, E. (2005). *Heidegger: l'introduction du nazisme dans la philosophie*. Paris: Albin Michel.
Franks, P. (2016). Fichte's Position: Anti-Subjectivism, Self-Awareness and Self-Location in the Space of Reasons. In G. Zöller and D. James, eds., *The Cambridge Companion to Fichte*. Cambridge: Cambridge University Press, 374–404.

References

Hemming, L. P. (2002). *Heidegger's Atheism: The Refusal of a Theological Voice*. Notre Dame: Notre Dame University Press.

Hengel, M. (1977). *Crucifixion in the Ancient World and the Folly of the Message of the Cross*. J. Bowden, trans. Philadelphia: Fortress Press.

Hirsch, E. (1978). Review of Martin Heidegger, Poetry, Language, and Thought. A. Hofstadter, trans. *Journal of the History of Philosophy* 16 (4), 489–492.

Husserl, E. (2019). *First Philosophy. Lectures 1923/24 and Related Texts from the Manuscripts (1920–1925)*. S. Luft and T. M. Naberhaus, trans. Dordrecht: Springer.

Kisiel, T. (1988). War der frühe Heidegger tatsächliche ein "christlicher Theologe?" In A. Gethmann-Siefert, ed. *Philosophie und Poesie: Otto Pöggeler zum 60 Geburtstag*. Stuttgart: Frommann-Holzboog, 59–75.

Kisiel, T. (1993). *The Genesis of Heidegger's Being and Time*. Berkeley: University of California Press.

Kisiel. T. (1994). *Heidegger (1920–1921) on Becoming a Christian: A Conceptual Picture Show*. In Ed. T. Kisiel and J. Van Buren, eds., *Reading Heidegger from the Start: Essays in His Earliest Thought*. Albany: SUNY Press, 175–192.

Macquarrie, J. (1965). *An Existentialist Theology: A Comparison of Heidegger and Bultmann*. London: SCM Press.

McGrath, S. (2006). *The Early Heidegger and Medieval Philosophy: Phenomenology for the Godforsaken*. Washington, DC: University of America Press.

McGrath, S. and Wiercinski, A., eds. (2010). *A Companion to Heidegger's Phenomenology of Religious Life*. Amsterdam: Brill.

Millgram, E. (2019). *John Stuart Mill and the Meaning of Life*. Oxford: Oxford University Press.

Mitchell, A. (2015). *The Fourfold: Reading the Late Heidegger*. Evanston: Northwestern University Press.

Nikelsburg, G. and VanderKam, J. (2001). *A Commentary on the Book of 1 Enoch, Chapters 1–36*. Minneapolis: Augsburg Fortress.

Polt, R. (2006). *The Emergency of Being: On Heidegger's Contributions to Philosophy*. Ithaca: Cornell University Press.

Polt, R. (2019). *Time and Trauma: Thinking through Heidegger in the Thirties*. London: Rowman and Littlefield.

Ricoeur, P. (1995). *Figuring the Sacred: Religion, Narrative, and Imagination*. M. Wallace, trans. Minneapolis: Fortress Press.

Rowland, C. (2002). *The Open Heaven: A Study of Apocalyptic in Judaism and Early Christianity*. Eugene: Wipf & Stock.

Sheehan, T. (1979). Heidegger's "Introduction to the Phenomenology of Religion," 1920–1921. *The Personalist* 60 (3), 312–324.

Thomson, I. D. (2005). *Heidegger on Ontotheology: Technology and the Politics and Education*. CUP.

Trawny, P. (2015). *Heidegger und der Mythos der jüdischen Weltverschwörung*. Frankfurt am Main: Klostermann.

Tucket, C., ed. (1983). *The Messianic Secret*. London: SPCK.

Van Buren, J. (1994). *The Young Heidegger: Rumor of the Hidden King*. Bloomington: Indiana University Press.

Wolfe, J. (2014). *Heidegger and Theology*. London: Bloomsbury.

Wrathall, M. (2021). *The Cambridge Heidegger Lexicon*. Cambridge: Cambridge University Press.

Wrathall, M. and Lambeth, M. (2011). Heidegger's Last God. *Inquiry* 54, 160–182.

Wrede, W. (1971). *The Messianic Secret*. J. C. G. Greig, trans. London: James Clark.

Zaborowski, H. (2010). *Eine Frage von Irre und Schuld? Martin Heidegger und der Nationalsozialismus*. Frankfurt am Main: Fischer Verlag.

Zimmerman, M. (1990). *Heidegger's Confrontation with Modernity: Technology, Politics, Art*. Bloomington: Indiana University Press.

Cambridge Elements

The Philosophy of Martin Heidegger

About the Editors

Filippo Casati
Lehigh University

Filippo Casati is an Assistant Professor at Lehigh University. He has published an array of articles in such venues as The British Journal for the History of Philosophy, Synthese, Logic et Analyse, Philosophia, Philosophy Compass and The European Journal of Philosophy. He is the author of Heidegger and the Contradiction of Being (Routledge) and, with Daniel O. Dahlstrom, he edited Heidegger on logic (Cambridge University Press).

Daniel O. Dahlstrom
Boston University

Daniel O. Dahlstrom, John R. Silber Professor of Philosophy at Boston University, has edited twenty volumes, translated Mendelssohn, Schiller, Hegel, Husserl, Heidegger, and Landmann-Kalischer, and authored Heidegger's Concept of Truth (2001), The Heidegger Dictionary (2013; second extensively expanded edition, 2023), Identity, Authenticity, and Humility (2017) and over 185 essays, principally on 18th-20th century German philosophy. With Filippo Casati, he edited Heidegger on Logic (Cambridge University Press).

About the Series

A continual source of inspiration and controversy, the work of Martin Heidegger challenges thinkers across traditions and has opened up previously unexplored dimensions of Western thinking. The Elements in this series critically examine the continuing impact and promise of a thinker who transformed early twentieth-century phenomenology, spawned existentialism, gave new life to hermeneutics, celebrated the truthfulness of art and poetry, uncovered the hidden meaning of language and being, warned of "forgetting" being, and exposed the ominously deep roots of the essence of modern technology in Western metaphysics. Concise and structured overviews of Heidegger's philosophy offer original and clarifying approaches to the major themes of Heidegger's work, with fresh and provocative perspectives on its significance for contemporary thinking and existence.

Cambridge Elements

The Philosophy of Martin Heidegger

Elements in the Series

Heidegger on Being Affected
Katherine Withy

Heidegger on Eastern/Asian Thought
Lin Ma

Heidegger on Poetic Thinking
Charles Bambach

Heidegger on Thinking
Lee Braver

Heidegger's Concept of Science
Paul Goldberg

Heidegger on Religion
Benjamin D. Crowe

A full series listing is available at: www.cambridge.org/EPMH

www.ingramcontent.com/pod-product-compliance
Ingram Content Group UK Ltd.
Pitfield, Milton Keynes, MK11 3LW, UK
UKHW022229250125
454010UK00008B/105